A Rough-I

Vashon and Maury Islands, Washington

Treat this book as you would the Scriptures —

A Rough-Hewn Guide to
Vashon and Maury Islands, Washington

GREG WESSEL

*Stories and Advice for Life on the Rock,
With Tips on How to Dress by Cindy Hoyt*

outskirts
press

Denver, Colorado

Contents

Introductions and Acknowledgements

AS THE TITLE might suggest, this is a rough-hewn guide designed to give both visitors and long-time residents an overview of life and living on Vashon and Maury Islands, with a little bit of helpful advice thrown in. To some, that might sound overly ambitious, given as Vashon residents are to thinking they know everything already. But others (hopefully including enough book purchasers to allow the authors to retire with their respective families in Tuscany) may find that this tiny compendium of insider's knowledge is just the ticket.

Some of these chapters have appeared in slightly different versions as articles in our local newspaper, *The Vashon-Maury Island Beachcomber*. I am greatly indebted to Editor Leslie Brown, and Arts Editor Liz Shepherd, for their guidance and patience in confronting my naïve efforts. They deal with goofballs like me all the time, and have never once gone off the deep end and thrown their typewriters out the window. At least, not that I can tell. It might be wise to check their typewriters for dents.

I want to thank Cindy Hoyt for two things: her amazing chapter on Vashon fashions, and her help in editing the rest of the text. I invited her to contribute the fashion chapter after she authored a very funny sketch on the same topic that was presented during a performance by *The Church of Great Rain*. During the performance, I realized that not only did I know nothing about dressing properly, but that Cindy did, and that she could write about it! If after reading her chapter you think that I even remotely resemble the typical Vashon male, I assure you that the resemblance is entirely coincidental. I grew up in Cincinnati in the 60s, and learned to dress in Missouri and Montana in the early 70s when I was a geology student and spelunker. Returning to my roots as I get older, I frequently adopt the same attire I did then, minus the used carbide and cave mud. This includes wearing a jean jacket covered with embroidered patches. Patch-covered jean jackets are not exactly haute couture on Vashon, but my wife Margaret lets me wear mine anyway, possibly because she is also a geologist and has been photographed wearing similar clothing. Fortunately, Cindy did not use my jacket as an example of what to avoid. But as an editor she did use some of my writing as an example of what to avoid, and for that I am grateful.

Something I need to mention before we get too far along is that Vashon and Maury Islands are labeled as if they are two islands, but they really aren't. This topic is addressed briefly elsewhere in this book, but for now you need to know that when I refer to "Vashon," I really mean both of the islands. I don't mean to offend anyone who lives on Maury Island by using this convention. I'll find another way to do that.

As a disclaimer, let me say that all of the topics in this volume have been favored with enough "real" information to give the prospective visitor a semi-decent travel guide, and to also give the prospective resident a taste (or warning) of what's to come. Current residents should already have figured most of this out. If they haven't, there's not much more I can do.

Lastly, I want to thank my wife, Margaret, for enduring our non-sensical world, keeping me humored, and laughing at most of my jokes. It's hard to keep laughing in the face of adversity, especially without medication, and I really admire her for it.

Greg Wessel
Blackmold Bluff, Vashon

"Facts" about the People's Republic of Vashon

THOSE OF YOU who read the newspaper or watch the news on television probably understand that actual facts are not valued in our society. Most Americans don't want to know the truth, which is why they read newspapers and watch television in the first place. Nevertheless, I feel compelled to include some real facts here. This is mostly because every guidebook I've examined starts out with facts like these, but perhaps more truthful. So let's do like Maria Von Trapp, and start at the very beginning. It's the very best place to start.

First Comes Naming (including what to call your Vashon dog)

IT'S SO BASIC that most of us have forgotten it, but you can't even talk about stuff unless you can name the things you're talking about. Even prehistoric man was aware of this. It was shortly after *Homo sapiens* evolved, and language was invented (probably by someone who had to ask the prehistoric equivalent of "Where is the bathroom?"), that people set about naming the things and the places around them.

At the dawn of history, most names were some variant of "Ugg," but with time names grew more complex. Both things and geographic places were given names that described their form and function. This naming convention has persisted to the present, and has been augmented (as histories accumulated) to include naming things and places in memory of events or people who came before.

It was in the 1740s that Carolus Linnaeus proposed his system of taxonomy, the science of naming and classifying things. The idea was to name only living things with names that are descriptive, using Latin. Each organism received a unique two-part name (the *genus* and *species*), but early scientists were occasionally puzzled by what they were trying to describe. By mistake, some non-living things were given scientific names, including rocks and a few chemical elements, and nearly the entire microscopic world went unnoticed until years later.

I think it is safe to say that before Linnaeus, people didn't know species existed. Certainly, folks were aware that there were different types of animals and plants, but most people didn't give much thought to why they were different, how they were different, or conversely how they were related. It was insight gained from naming and classification that led to Charles Darwin's revelations a century later.

The grouping of organisms by their similarities suggested family relationships that were not apparent otherwise. Scientists organized living creatures into kingdoms (animals, plants, and things that are neither), phyla (subgroups of kingdoms), classes (subgroups of phyla), orders, families, etc., with the smallest divisions being genus and species. Birds were grouped with other birds (and later dinosaurs), mammals were grouped together because they produce milk, attorneys were grouped with other reptiles, and lobsters were grouped together with spiders, which is why I won't eat lobsters. But each individual type of organism got its own distinctive two-part name. For example, dogs were called *Canis familiaris*, which pretty much is Latin for *Friendly Dog*. Wolves (thought to be related to dogs), are *Canis lupus (Nasty Dog That Will Eat You)*. Coyotes are *Canis latrans (Cute Dog That Will Nevertheless Eat The Housecat)*. And so on.

On thing that is constant in science is change, and in 1993, dogs were reclassified as *Canis lupus familiaris*, a subspecies of the gray wolf, by the Smithsonian Institution and the American Society of Mammalogists. They did this because *"overwhelming evidence from behavior, vocalizations, morphology, and molecular biology led to the contemporary scientific understanding that a single species, the gray wolf, is the common ancestor for all breeds of domestic dogs."* Personally, I think dogs deserve their own species, if for no other reason than to honor their years of service to mankind. Just think of all the squirrels you'd have to chase, the stale leftovers you'd have to choke down, and the balls you'd have to fetch if Fido wasn't there to do it for you. No lousy wolf is going to provide such service.

Another purpose in giving creatures names like these was to differentiate them from other organisms. In theory, each species would be different enough that it could not mate successfully with other species, even those that bear the same genus name. For example, *Canis lupus* typically will not mate with *Canis latrans,* at least not willingly. And *Homo sapiens* certainly cannot mate with *Equus caballus,* although there have been some people in the town of Enumclaw, Washington, who have tried.

Of course, there are exceptions. For instance, there is the Eastern Coyote, which is a wolf-coyote hybrid. Having a parent who was a wolf, the Eastern Coyote is one honkin' coyote that is fortunately still a little reluctant to cross paths with humans. It is a Western Coyote on steroids, and it's spreading through the northeastern US and Canada. The Eastern Coyote is a good example of a hybrid that formed probably because of some environmental stress such as loss of habitat or a reduction in the number of available mates. For those of us who went to college, it's sort of like what happens when you graduate and have to move off-campus.

Recent discoveries have shown that the genus *Homo* is no stranger to similar hybridizations. Early in 2010, it was reported that modern man (or woman) mated in the past with what used to be thought a separate species, *Homo neanderthalensis.* That Neanderthals have interbred with "modern" humans does not at all surprise me. One only has to look at members of the Republican Party these days to see the resemblance.

Naming is so primary to science that some scientists spend their entire careers doing nothing else, much to the dismay of their families (and their genus and species). In the nineteenth century, there were even two scientists (okay, they were geologists) who got into a fossil hunting war just so they each could claim more discoveries than the other.

The rivalry between Edward Drinker Cope (of the Academy of Natural Sciences in Philadelphia) and Othniel Charles Marsh (of the Peabody Museum of Natural History at Yale) sparked what some folks have called the Bone Wars, also known as the "Great Dinosaur Rush." Each of them fielded exploration teams that scoured the west for fossil sites, and along the way they used underhanded methods to try to out-compete the other in the field, including bribery, theft, and destruction of fossils. They also attacked each other in scientific publications, seeking to ruin their opponent's credibility and reduce his funding. Both Cope and Marsh found lots of fossils and began to name the creatures before they had a chance to sort out which bones belonged to what.

Relations between these two pioneering explorers had started out as cordial, but early on Marsh had the audacity to point out that Cope had reassembled an *Elasmosaurus* skeleton with the skull placed on the end of the tail. Unfortunately, this was just after Cope's reconstruction was announced in print. Marsh's observation was thus not especially timely, and served to fuel the growing competition. At one point, they each gave the same dinosaur a different name, and it took literally decades to sort it all out. Ever hear of the dinosaur *Brontosaurus*? Forget that name...it's now called *Apatosaurus*, thanks to one of these gentlemen.

Geographic features are another story entirely. As mentioned above, place names are also commonly descriptive (particularly if they have Native American origins), but they can memorialize a person (Washington, DC), an event (Intercourse, PA), or another place that was special to the first settlers (New York, NY). What is different about place names is that there is no convention for naming places, and place names usually change with each succeeding wave of "settlers."

The people who live in an area typically give names to their places. When new people show up, the names may be changed, often before any of the new people actually stick around. That is why so few place names in the United States remain that are Native American in origin.

Consider, for example, the names of our two islands. Vashon and Maury were each named for sailors (British and American, respectively) who apparently never set foot on the islands. And does anyone who is not a historical society member know from where Dockton got its name? Okay, so my wife pointed out that many people know that, but I'm thinking that the no-longer-used Native American names probably would make more sense to most of us today, provided we could pronounce them.

I stated above that there is no convention for naming places or geographic features. While that is technically correct, there are some types of names you can no longer use because they are either indiscrete or politically incorrect. It was not that long ago that the mapping division of the U. S. Geological Survey set about "correcting" place names that originated from some of the earliest European explorers to penetrate the wilderness of America in the 18th and 19th centuries. These men were both lonely and far from the constraints of civilization, sort of like if you go to college at an engineering school, and so their place names sometimes commemorated parts of the female anatomy. The U.S.G.S. could not change them all (the Grand Tetons are a good example) but places like "Nellie's Nipple" (in California) were either left unlabeled or quietly renamed on some maps. Oddly, not many peaks were named after male anatomical features, at least not without a lot of accompanying laughter.

The naming frenzy for living organisms as well as geographic features continues to the present day. Scientists are looking for new organisms all the time just so they can claim naming rights, and the names no longer need be Latin descriptions of the organism's characteristics. If I were to discover a new species of Vashon dog, for instance, I could legitimately name it *Canis gregii* (Greg's Dog). In fact, we have a canine in our house that I have already named *Canis bubbyi vashonensis* (Bubby the Dog who lives on Vashon). But don't tell my wife, because she thinks his name is simply Bubby.

The type specimen for *Canis bubbyi vashonensis* in his natural habitat.

Geology (rocks, the universe, and everything)

THE GEOLOGY OF Vashon and Maury Islands is the most fascinating topic that I will address in this book. With respect to its impact on mankind and human development, everything else pales in comparison. Few people would argue with me about that, at least to my face. Coincidentally, geology is also the only topic about which I am truly qualified to write. I could get really technical in this chapter and use big words like "diagenesis" and "ophiolite." Instead, I'll make it simple, assuming you'll take it all for granite anyway (ha ha).

Vashon is home to several geologic features that you should know about, particularly if you are going to live here for any extended period of time. Landslides are the most important of these, and there's an entire chapter devoted to landslides, but before we can discuss those features, we need to review the basics. Assuming that you know as much about our Earth's history as I know about podiatry, we'll begin with a primer on the origin of the universe and our planet, mainly because I couldn't figure out where else to put it. Following that, we'll review the geology of the Pacific Northwest, reasoning that it's important to know a little bit about the ground you walk on, if only to avoid stepping in something you'll regret.

Before you can think much about geology, you have to consider the vastness of geologic time in relation to time as experienced by humans. When geologists talk about mountains being built or glaciers advancing, normal folks sometimes imagine these events as occurring fast enough to be caught in the act outside their bedroom window. But except for some rapid events that are relatively small-scale (such as landslides), major geologic changes often are accomplished over millions of years.

I think it was because I was born in southwestern Ohio that I learned to appreciate the vastness of geologic time even as a young child. Southwestern Ohio is home to the world's second greatest concentration of fossils, lagging just behind the United States Congress. The geologists among us would say they are marine fossils (meaning fossils of animals that lived in the sea) from the Late Ordovician Period (meaning they are about 450 million years old). The rolling hills of southern Ohio look nothing like the bottom of the sea, and yet they used to be just that about 450 million years ago.

A million years is a long time, I bet you are thinking, and we're talking 450 of them! If it's hard for you to appreciate such an immense passage of time, think for a minute about when your relatives drop in for a visit. Do you know how long it seems before they decide to leave? Multiply that by 10 and you can begin to understand.

Few of us need to worry about geologic time in our day-to-day activities. Instead, our existence is governed by the rapid rotation of the Earth in its orbit around the Sun, and on Vashon also by the ferry schedule. This does not mean that you need a mechanical time-piece to tell you when to race to the ferry. For instance, after years of walking around in the woods, during only a few of which I could be classified as "lost," I have learned to tell the time of day from the angle of the Sun above or below the horizon. When checked against actual timepieces, I am usually off by no more than 15 minutes. That's better than the Metro buses!

One might argue that no matter how much we enjoy reading and learning about our local geology, there is nothing more important than the BIG question of how the universe is put together and how our Earth was created. This is, in fact, a question that has been asked repeatedly since the beginning of humankind, if not before, and also one that has been "definitively" answered just as many times, by men and women of both science and religion. I personally solved this problem 14 times just in the last month. Unfortunately, each of my solutions has proven incorrect, but that's why we have the concept of multiple working hypotheses.

More than a few theories of the origin of the universe (and by extension, the Earth) have been put forward by mankind. Some have been incredibly creative, incorporating gods for everything from taking out the garbage to visiting your in-laws. But I am not a theolo-gian. My cosmology (and by extension, my geology) begins with the observations of Galileo, who put on a really good pair of glasses and noticed that the Earth revolves around the Sun.

Today there is little agreement on the number, sex, or existence of gods in any form. Even though we made it through the "Age of Reason," people are still daft enough to kill each other over their competing myths, and that includes "educated" Americans.

Mythical beliefs are common among humans, including many people who insist they are not religious. For example, there seems to be an inverse relationship between belief in official deities and be-lief in the existence of mythical creatures. Evidence for this includes many of our younger citizens, who avoid churches like the plague and instead spend hours of each day working out the intricate relationships of a fantasy world through a video game. Some of these same people learn to speak Klingon.

But many of us have accepted the observations of our astronomers and other people with good eyesight. We can see and accept the fact that there are planets and moons and stars and black holes and white holes and galaxies of every shape and color. There are billions of stars in our galaxy and probably billions of galaxies, all moving away from a central point in space, which by my calculation should be somewhere a little south of Cleveland. And the Earth is far from being the only planet likely to host carbon-based life forms.

The descendants of Galileo tell us that around 13.5 billion years ago, the entire universe we know started out as a tiny mass of something about the size of a Buick two-door coupe (referred to as the "singularity") that exploded in what we now call the Big Bang. Using lots of complex astronomical observations and mathematical equations of the type that gave me headaches in college, lots of people smarter than me have worked out the history of the universe from the moment of the Big Bang until today, and extrapolated into the future.

Geologists understand the passage of large quantities of time, but typically we think of just the last two billion years or so, and often just the last few hundred million. Our Eras and Periods and Epochs span millions of years during which not much happened that anyone (except a geologist) would write home about.

The timeline according to particle physics is a little different. In the first one second (yes...one second) after the Big Bang, there are FOUR epochs! The universe expanded exponentially and quarks and anti-quarks flew around and the four forces were created. The quarks become confined within hadrons and hydrogen nuclei were created, all in just one second.

And then things start to slow down. The first stars begin to shine 100 million years after the Big Bang. The first galaxy formed at 600 million years. Our galaxy formed, with our Sun and the Earth, about 9.1 billion years after the Big Bang, roughly 4.5 billion years ago.

If things keep going this way, the universe will continue to cool and expand and stars will cease forming in several trillion years. This marks the beginning of what they call The Degenerate Era. I'd rather not describe The Degenerate Era here, but you can rest assured that it has nothing to do with the legal profession or politics. Fox News may figure prominently, however.

At this point, you may be asking "Just what are rocks?" Or better yet, "What is matter and energy? And what is this String Theory I keep hearing about? Is this the same as the G-String Theory that you've written about elsewhere?" No, it's not, but there is a similarity in that both theories rely upon the existence of strings. In one case, I'd better not say more because I think my wife might read this far into this book. In the other case, the basic building blocks of sub-atomic particles are thought to be little energy strings that I can't begin to describe. But my references say that protons and neutrons and hadrons are made of smaller particles called quarks, and quarks can be made of hypothetical one-dimensional "strings," infinitely small building-blocks that have only the dimension of length, but not height or width. String theory also suggests that the universe is made up of as many as eleven dimensions. We only perceive four dimensions (unless you're a fan of golden oldies, and then there's the Fifth Dimension), but String Theory supports the presence of more that we can't detect.

These "strings" vibrate in multiple dimensions, and depending on how they vibrate, they might be seen in our three-dimensional space as matter, light, or gravity. It is the vibration of the string that determines whether it appears to be matter or energy, and every form of matter or energy is the result of the vibration of strings. Are you confused yet? Yeah, me, too.

As with any simple observation that is taken too far, the theorists ran into a problem. Other versions of the String Theory equations were discovered, so that there were eventually five different String Theories, all of which appeared to be correct. I think this is almost funny considering that the theories postulate multiple universes....so why not different versions of the same theory? Of COURSE they'd all be correct! Duh! But some scientists were not comfortable with this and eventually one of them (Edward Witten) came up with a unifying theory that tied all of them together. His M-Theory (for membrane, matrix, mother, monster, mystery or magic), relying on even more incomprehensible mathematics, asserts that strings are really one-dimensional slices of a two-dimensional membrane vibrating in 11-dimensional space.

M-Theory is still under development (somewhat like the electric car), but the structure of the mathematics has been established and it is in agreement with all the other theories as well as our observations. Unfortunately, it's hard to test the theory without measuring the invisible dimensions, and they don't call them invisible for nothing. But what is visible are some of the products resulting from the creation of the universe and the organization of matter and energy through time, including the elements that were formed inside generations of stars and that now make up everything on and within the Earth, including rocks.

The Earth is a rocky sphere that is made up of layers of differing composition, sort of like a golf ball. If, like me, you've ever cut a golf ball in half, I'm sure you'll never try THAT again! But unlike the outside of the golf ball (which is a thin layer of plastic), the outside of the Earth is a thin crust of cooled rocks, dirt, and water. Just a bit below the crust, it gets really hot and the "rocks" become like Silly Putty. At some levels, they are more liquid; at other levels, they are less so. That's about all you need to know about what's deep inside the Earth, except that the deeper you go, the heavier the elements get. When you get to the core, it's mostly really heavy elements like iron, nickel, uranium, gold and stuff like that. It's my opinion (yet to be indicated by any actual data) that at the very center of the Earth is a solid gold and platinum sphere just waiting to be mined. If we could just drill that deep (rumor has it that BP was trying that in the Gulf of Mexico), precious metals would come up molten and could be cast directly into ingots. Unfortunately, no one else agrees with me about that, but they do agree that the light elements (silicon, sodium, oxygen, etc.) are concentrated near the surface, and many of the lightest elements are in the continents themselves.

The continents are like rafts riding on the sort-of-molten "mantle," which is the layer just under the crust. Think of them as the marshmallows on your hot chocolate. The oceans are where the upper mantle has become exposed, and a crust has formed that is different from the composition of the continents. Think of oceanic crust as being the skin that forms on your hot chocolate if you don't drink it right away. Being composed of light compounds, you can't push the marshmallows down into the mantle, but you can move them around and crush them together (where mountains are made) and pull them apart (where rift valleys are made). You can also slide one past another, with a fault separating the two (as in California).

The Pacific Northwest is one area where an oceanic plate is being pushed under a continental plate. Just offshore, there is a deep trench that marks the location of this, which is called a subduction zone. The edge of the continent, meaning western Washington, is being compressed and uplifted as the collision proceeds. Deep underground, parts of the oceanic plate are melting and rising through the continental plate, creating a string of volcanoes in an arc that parallels the offshore trench.

As you might imagine, we have more than a few earthquakes in this area, some deep along the subduction zone and some shallow within the overriding crust. I have experienced two in my 13 years living here, and they are WAY cool, let me tell you! Buildings bump and shake, windows rattle, and if you position that horrible vase that Aunt Mildred gave you on the mantle just so, you can watch it drop and smash into a zillion pieces. Too bad it wasn't insured, you can tell her.

Scientists like me know where earthquakes might occur because we are keeping track of where they happened before. So if you don't like earthquakes, stay away from where they have happened in the past. Sadly, those areas that are most earthquake-prone are also the most beautiful locations (like Vashon) and where all the best parties are held. In the middle of Kansas, you'll be safe from earthquakes and probably bored silly.

If that isn't enough to keep you interested, you should know that only 10,000 years ago or so, Vashon was covered with thousands of feet of solid ice! During the Pleistocene, several pulses of continental glaciation filled the Puget Sound Basin with lobes of ice moving south from Canada. These foreign intruders brought with them gravel, sand, and silt that was deposited in layers throughout the area, covering our native home-grown rocks and burying them under mounds of debris. Just about all of the rocks and soils you see on Vashon, or for that matter around Seattle, originated from these glaciers.

At last count, there were no active volcanoes on Vashon, but there are some nearby. In eastern King County, there are also coal mines that occasionally collapse and swallow cars and homes. Call me an adrenaline junkie, but I want to live where there are earthquakes and landslides and volcanoes and collapsing mines. That's why I live near Seattle, home to the largest single concentration of geologic hazards in the world. And boy, can we party!

Climate (it's raining again)

IF YOU HAVE to inquire about the climate in the Seattle area and on Vashon, you clearly haven't been listening or are from someplace far away that doesn't get *Frasier* reruns. For those people, let me say it's misty or rainy much of the time. When it's not raining, it's foggy. But if the sun actually comes out because of a once-a-century planetary alignment, comet impact, or other rare occurrence, it's pretty nice. In fact, it's danged nice.

It never gets very cold here, and it never gets very hot. I'd be right roughly 85% of the time if I predicted the weather to be cloudy with temperatures between 40 and 65 degrees Fahrenheit. Far be if from me to gloat, but this beats the records held by all of the forecasters at the National Weather Service, who surprisingly get paid for their predictions.

As a result of the unchanging climate, lots of people wear the same clothes all year round, with short breaks on laundry days and sometimes not even then. I think it is also this constancy in weather that leads to the laid-back attitude commonly attached to islanders, here and elsewhere. I contend that living on "island time" can refer to life on Vashon just as much as it refers to life in Hawaii, Bermuda, and the Virgin Islands. Our hired help doesn't show up on time, and if invited to parties, we never arrive at the appointed hour. Think of us as Polynesians wearing fleeces.

That said, there is an interesting difference in climate from one side of Vashon-Maury to the other. The west side of Vashon Island gets more rain than the eastern end of Maury Island, up to 10 inches more per year. You might not think that is much, but 10 inches is 25% more. Still, it's hard to tell the difference unless you look at subtle differences in plant distribution. There are no cacti growing on the west side of Vashon, for example.

Flora (the good, the bad, and the prickly)

I COULD WRITE a lot about plants here if I knew much about them, but plants to a geologist are like clothes to a voyeur. They just get in the way of seeing what interests you. However, there are a couple of fascinating things I've learned about plants over the years, and by "couple" I mean exactly two.

The first interesting thing has to do with the way they eat. Most people think that plants "eat" by using sunlight to convert water and carbon dioxide to sugars through a process called photosynthesis. If God should be proud of anything, it should be for inventing photosynthesis, but even God makes errors. For instance, photosynthesis is great during the day, but at night, you would think that plants can't eat! We animals can find the refrigerator and consume a quart of ice cream at two in the morning even if the refrigerator light is burned out, but the poor plants have to wait until morning to get their sugar! Or so you'd think unless you knew like I do that plants also *respire*...

that is they breathe in oxygen during the night and breathe out carbon dioxide, using up nutrients they created during photosynthesis. During they day they act like plants and during the night they act like animals, which could be said about many of us.

Some plants also get their food by wrapping around animals and slowly digesting them. I really really hope this does not include any of the plants in my yard.

The second interesting thing I have learned about plants is that flowers are sexual organs. I think this is funny because we give flowers to people in whom we are romantically interested. Nothing says love like a handful of colorful cut-off sexual organs for your sweetie!

With respect to plants on Vashon, there are a lot of them here and they fall into two categories: desirable native plants that used to populate this entire region, and evil invasive non-native plants that are slowly taking over.

Sadly, Vashon has been totally denuded by logging several times. If you stop by the History Museum and look at pictures from the early days, the first thing you'll notice is the absence of trees. Early loggers didn't concern themselves much with forest management. Their modus operandi, as the mystery writers would say, was "slash, slash, burn." As a result, few loggers planted replacement trees. When they did, the trees were mostly Douglas Firs. In addition, large areas of the island were under cultivation until about 40 years ago, which pretty much eliminates all forms of vegetation at least once a year (during plowing). Since then, the abandoned fields have grown up with Red Alder and Himalayan Blackberry.

A hint to the location of past cultivation or clear cutting is forest cover that is predominately one species. If you see nothing but Red Alder with blackberries and a few spindly evergreens, then you likely are looking at a site that was a farm in the 1930s. Or you could be looking at a site that was totally cleared 40 to 50 years ago and has been left alone since. If you see mostly one species of tree, no matter what it is, there's a problem.

There are a number of good plant identification books out there for those of you with not much to do. For everyone else, let me point out that you can often tell the good plants from the evil ones by their names. Western Red Cedar is from the western United States. English Ivy and English Holly are not. Douglas Fir (possibly named after Douglas McArthur, Frederick Douglas, or Douglas Fairbanks, Sr.) is a proud patriot. Scotch Broom and Himalayan Blackberry are not.

King County maintains a list of undesirables, including some you are required to kill on sight. Seriously. But they don't seem to worry much about the most prevalent invaders, principally because they are so widespread that botanists don't think there is any way to stop them. Fortunately, I know better.

The four main invaders you should keep on your radar, and that I've already mentioned, are: English Ivy, English Holly, Scotch Broom, and Himalayan Blackberries. You can find these practically every-where you look. Just kill them. Don't ask questions; just do it.

Of course, if you're on someone else's property, you should prob-ably clear it with them first. You could introduce yourself as a student of silviculture (tree growing) and point out that their Holly trees are infested with a fungus that can be spread to dogs and humans, caus-ing a slow and lingering death. That this is not actually true is of little consequence in the fight against plant-based terrorists.

The Ivy is strangling our trees and the Holly is displacing our gentle native plants, and yet few care enough to do anything about it. That's why those of us who are concerned citizens have to get tough! Those of you who are armchair ivy slayers can still help by supporting a new effort that was recently established called "Ivy-Free Vashon." Two island women, Sarah Driggs and Cynthia Young, started the group to mobilize folks and rid Vashon of ivy forever. Clearly, they've more than a little work to do, so you should support them however you can.

With respect to Holly, a word of warning: it is known to masquer-ade as Oregon Grape. Oregon Grape is a smaller bush with similar leaves that is one of our prized natives, and it can be confused with Holly, which could lead to a massacre of innocents. Holly grows much larger, and Holly twigs and branches are smooth and green, whereas Oregon Grape twigs and branches are brown and rougher. Also, Oregon Grape leaves are thinner and more flexible. So when you are about to uproot or cut down something that looks like Holly, make sure it really is.

These are not green trees; rather these are Alder trees in the winter that are covered with ivy. Notice how they are poised to fall on the power line. Many winter power outages are caused by the falling of ivy-covered trees.

Despite being mentioned in Christmas carols (remember that the British also brought us slavery, taxation without representation, and something called Spotted Dick), there is nothing gentle about Holly, so get out your axe and murder some. And while you are chopping away, don't forget to collect some firewood for the winter. This is the other thing about plants on Vashon that you need to know: which wood is the best for your fireplace.

Lots of people prefer Pacific Madrona for firewood. Also called "Madrone" (in California) and "Arbutus" (in Canada, where they don't even use the same kind of money we do), the real name of this species is *Arbutus menziesii*. The names Madrone and Madrona come from *madrono*, the Spanish word for strawberry tree, because of its resemblance to a Mediterranean strawberry tree. This, of course, means that the Canadians are using a more accurate name for the species, but I will not mention that here.

The Madrona is a large smooth-trunk tree with oblate leaves that grows on dry slopes. The wood burns hot and long if you can actually get it into pieces small enough to fit in your fireplace. The trick with Madrona is that it's heavy, tough, and really hard to split. I think it's actually made of something like titanium, but I'm not sure. Madrona trunks were reportedly used to construct early versions of the Minuteman missile. And don't bother to think about splitting it when it's wet. Even when it's dry, you're going to need extra help in the form of Conan the Barbarian.

Other folks prefer Douglas Fir. Doug Fir is common everywhere and grows like a weed, adding up to six feet of height in a single year. The wood is moderately splittable...if that's a word...and it burns well. I don't like it because it also pops and cracks, sending hot embers onto the rug upon which I recline with my wife and a glass of wine. Not that I do that often, but it only takes one hot ember in a sensitive spot to cure you of Doug Fir.

My favorite firewood is Red Alder. You can split Alder by looking at it cross-eyed; it's that easy. In fact, you can have fun seeing just how thin a piece of Alder you can split off of a cut log. You could even turn this activity into a family competition that will get the kids outside and give them some exercise, Tom Sawyer-fashion. A few of them may lose a thumb, but opposable digits are highly overrated, and in later years it will keep them from texting while driving.

Another side benefit of using Alder is that if you cut one down, you can replace it with a small Fir or Cedar and pat yourself on the back for lessening the nitrate runoff in nearby streams. Yes, it's true that Alder stands are a natural source of nitrate in streams. The nitrate finds its way (mostly by going downhill) into marine waters, where it contributes to the creation of "dead zones," including in Quartermaster Harbor. I don't know why this is, but I assume it has something to do with chemistry. Other nearby dead zones, such as Des Moines and Kent, cannot blame Alders for their woes. But they might get away with blaming the trees in the sleepy hamlet of Black Diamond.

If you don't think about trees much during the summer, I can assure you that you will think about them every day during the winter. That is because during any storm, and even on some calm sunny days, a number of our branch-endowed friends are likely to decide to lie down over a power line. During one big storm a couple of years ago, there were something like 75 simultaneously downed power lines island-wide. Our house was without power for five days. Fortunately, we have natural gas as well as electricity, so we could boil water for cooking, tea and baths. We drank tea like crazy and ate lots of pasta. I even took hot water in a thermos to our elderly neighbor every morning for her breakfast, but baths were another matter. Our kitchen pots quickly proved too small to bathe in, so we wound up taking showers at the YMCA, which has since closed. Something like this happens once or twice each winter.

I wrote a song about one our typical winter storms, which you can sing to the tune of Johnny Cash's "Folsom Prison Blues." For some strange reason, Capitol Records did not return my phone calls about this:

I hear the chain saws runnin',
They're runnin' round the bend,
And I ain't had a shower,
Since I don't know when.
I'm stuck in Vashon winter,
Not where I wanna be,
'Cause we'd still have hot water,
'Cept fer that fallin' tree.

My neighbor's lights are shinin',
His generator's hot,
But he won't 'vite me over,
'Cause smellin' good I'm not.
I'm stuck in Vashon winter,
Not where I wanna be,
My fireplace is roarin',
But I can only make tea.

I see the lights at Southworth,
The people warm and glad,
Reminds me of my buddy,
And that extra beer he had.
We're stuck in Vashon winter,
Just where we wanna be,
Sittin' by the fire,
And havin' two or three.

So if you plan to visit us during the winter, you might want to bring a non-electric musical instrument, your singing voice, a really really big stew pot, and an extra box of candles. Be assured that bathing in the kitchen is limited to very close friends and family, and we will not use the same water for pasta most of the time.

Fauna (tasty and annoying, with two aside dishes)

IT IS INTERESTING to me that when humans think about animals, they classify them first into two types: animals that are likely to be seen only on the dinner table, and animals that are likely to be seen only on television. The two groups rarely overlap in our minds. Of course, this is an overly simplistic approach to animal classification. In reality, there is a third group: animals that are neither on the dinner table nor on television, but that you'd like to keep out of your garden. It is the members of this third group that you are most likely to encounter on Vashon.

On Vashon, we also have an abundance of bird species that don't seem to fall into any of the above categories. Most of the birds I can't recognize, but this is why we have books on bird identification. There is a good one titled *The Birds of Vashon Island* (by Ed Swan) that is available in local bookstores. There are a lot of big birds, including Eagles, Crows, and Pileated Woodpeckers. There are also a lot of small birds that never sit still long enough to identify and that eat my birdseed so fast, it's as if they own stock in the seed company.

I'm not going to say anything about the marine fauna living in the waters around us. None of them actually live "on" the island, but it is fun to watch the Orcas and whales when they decide to show up. I was out walking the dog once on KVI Beach when a Gray Whale surfaced about 25 yards offshore. The whale's exhale surprised the heck out of me, but Bubby the Dog didn't even notice. He was too busy eating a dead crab.

I'm also not going to say anything about the domesticated fauna, including dogs (of which there are many), cats, ferrets, cows, horses, llamas, sheep, chickens or pigs. Regarding goats, you should just for fun check out Rent-A-Ruminant, LLC on the web. Islander Tammy Dunakin has a herd of goats that she hires out for brush clearing. They will happily eat and completely remove ivy, blackberries, and all other undesirable brush, as well as junked cars, dilapidated buildings and piles of trash. Okay, so I exaggerated a bit, but they are so efficient at brush clearing that they were featured on *The Colbert Report* as an example of a company that is destroying America by taking jobs away from American landscaping contractors. "Horny goats head to a Department of Defense nuclear sub base after stealing all the landscaping jobs," says the headline. There is a link to a very funny video on their web site that shows a goat's paw pressing the launch button of a nuclear missile.

But if you want to be afraid of something, it's not goats. You should be wary of the two most common species of mammalian wildlife on the island, raccoons and deer.

Despite their cute markings and reputation for cleanliness, raccoons are vicious creatures that can tear the head off of a duck while simultaneously tipping over a trash can. They are voracious eaters who will eat vegetables and fruit, and will attack mammals their own size. I even know of one island contractor (honestly) who was attacked by a raccoon as he examined the crawl space under a house. Fortunately, he lived to tell the tale, but was clearly shaken by the experience. I know of other people whose dogs attacked raccoons and came away seriously bloodied. Raccoons are not to be messed with, and should never be fed. They are not cute harmless little creatures. Let them get their own damn food, is my opinion.

Deer are another story. If you have any desire to garden, any desire at all, just forget it unless you are willing to surround your garden with a sturdy eight-foot-tall deer fence. Otherwise, they will eat everything you plant and then some. They will even eat ferns, small cedar trees, and blackberries (perhaps they are related to goats), and of course everything you are trying to grow. In fact, I think they identify which plants are being nurtured by humans and target those plants for consumption.

Deer also hang out along the roadways in the evening and will spontaneously jump in front of automobiles. As one who knows from experience (I totaled my wife's Honda Odyssey by hitting a deer), plowing broadside into a doe or buck is not for the faint-hearted. In fact, I think it is true that most traffic accidents on Vashon involve deer. Whether the deer were drinking, I cannot say.

If it were up to me, I would work for formal recognition of the third category of fauna (Animals That You Want To Keep Out Of Your Garden) so that we could begin to apply for grants to study and sterilize the deer and raccoons. I'm only partly kidding about that. But other folks across the country have their own goofy ideas about how animals should be viewed, and some of these people have been rather convincing.

For example, Herman Kahn, the famous futurist and military statistician, had a few things to say about the classification of animals. Perhaps you have never heard of Herman Kahn, and so I suspect that some background information is in order.

Born in New Jersey in 1922, Kahn spent World War II as a telephone lineman in Burma, but he gained little experience with actual warfare. He went to college after the war and was recruited by his friends to work at the Rand Corporation. Kahn became involved with the development of the hydrogen bomb, and he worked closely with Edward Teller, Hans Bethe, and others at the Lawrence Livermore Laboratory. His major contributions were several strategies he developed during the Cold War to contemplate nuclear warfare using applications of game theory.

Herman Kahn (1922-1983) who seems to be explaining to Congress how he saved money getting to the top secret hearing by thumbing a ride with the Soviet attaché. This photo is of a low quality because it was reportedly taken with a tie clasp camera by the French ambassador.

In 1960, as Cold War tensions were near their peak, Kahn published *On Thermonuclear War*. His theories presented in that book were based on two premises, that nuclear war was *feasible*, since the United States and the Soviet Union had massive nuclear arsenals aimed at each other, and that it was *winnable*. Whether hundreds of millions died or nations merely lost a few cities, life would go on, he argued, which was contrary to then-prevailing doomsday scenarios. To believe otherwise would mean that deterrence was unnecessary, and I think probably he had a point there. Why have all these weapons if you couldn't use them safely? What mattered was that we had to have a viable *second*-strike capability. This was the genesis of MAD, the policy of Mutually Assured Destruction. We could keep paying for these weapons provided that we, together with the Russians who subscribed to the same policy, had enough to destroy both countries and by extension the rest of the planet. No one would dare attack us! If we didn't have enough missles to win after enduring a crippling first strike, then we were sitting ducks, and the Pentagon could certainly not allow that.

Kahn's thesis may have been the greatest achievement for the military-industrial complex since the invention of gunpowder. This policy and the economic engine it drove were so powerful that they existed well into the Reagan Administration. Fortunately, during the Reagan Administration, the Russians finally got cable and began to watch MTV and other bootleg shows, which I believe is what really brought an end to both MAD and the evil Soviet empire.

I witnessed this myself (really) when I was in southern Russia in the early 1990s. The local administrators were incredibly proud of their cable hookup and the fact that they could watch *Benny Hill*. I actually watched *Benny Hill* with a group of them after sitting in a steam bath (banya). Afterwards, we sat around a low table, wrapped in white sheets, drinking vodka, Fanta orange soda and imported German beer, and eating sausage, tomatoes and cucumbers while we watched old *Benny Hill* reruns. I was occasionally called upon to explain the jokes to my translator, who did his best to translate the intent of the humor. A lot of it needed no translation.

A number of western shows were available in Volgograd by the time I got there. It was funny that the Russians preferred British humour over American humor, but there were other American shows that found their way into the former Soviet empire and that generated a following. I was lucky that no one during my travels through Russia ever asked me who shot JR, because I would not have known the answer.

In my later visits to Russia, the most popular TV show was a Mexican soap opera called *Santa Barbara*. People were glued to their sets night after night, which is similar to the way Americans have been living since *Dark Shadows* first appeared on television in the 1960s.

Call me a cynic if you will, but I'm not the only one who has noticed that television can be used to distract the populace. The following quotes are from the *St. Petersburg Times* (Russia, not Florida) of February 17, 2009, in an article entitled *How Soap Operas Can Save Us*:

> "We clearly underestimate the significance of soap operas in our lives. If a monument to the liberal economic reforms of 1992 is ever built, the main figure should be a hero from a popular Mexican or Brazilian soap opera. Since Russians were glued to their television sets, never missing a single show, they neither had the time nor the emotional strength to stage an uprising against the government.

> "...*The Rich Also Cry* was the name of one of the first Mexican soaps shown on Russian television. It was precisely this series that kept Russians in their warm living rooms in front of the television and not rebelling on the streets against the government's shock therapy."

It was not my intent here to suggest that the current proliferation of reality TV shows (including *America's Next Top Model*) is in any way an attempt to divert the public's attention away from real problems like environmental degradation, poverty, corporate greed, and corrupt politicians. It is true that the number of reality shows did reach a peak during the Bush Administration, but we had distractions before then as well. For years, Americans have relied upon alcohol, marijuana, sex, Hollywood, and professional football (and combinations thereof) to provide an escape from reality. How many more distractions could we possibly need? Instead, it was my intent to note that prior to the distractions of television both here and abroad, there were more than a few people who were not happy with Herman Kahn.

Due to his clear articulation of the most brutal possibilities, Kahn came to be thought of as a monster. Few of the conventional downsides of nuclear war really bothered him. Fallout, for example, was a temporary inconvenience. Most people would not be affected by birth defects due to radiation, and contaminated food could be eaten by the elderly, who were going to kick off soon anyway. So why worry? We could beat the Russians and come out ahead if only we had fallout shelters and could bomb them into oblivion.

If you've ever seen Stanley Kubrick's movie *Dr. Strangelove*, you've seen the influence of Herman Kahn. He reportedly gave Kubrick the idea for the Doomsday Machine.

As nuclear tensions eased during the 1970s, Kahn found that he'd soon be out of a job. So he turned his attention to futurism and speculations about coming disasters. Kahn's opinion of the future was anything but gloomy. He held that capitalism and technology held the potential for nearly boundless growth and ultimately the colonization of space, presumably with Republicans who supported Ronald Reagan. The *Global 2000* report came out at roughly the same time, which did not see such a rosy future. The country became polarized, much as it is today. Few people occupied the middle ground, or were accurate (at least in public), and exaggerations were as common as mosquitoes in Alaska.

It was during this time that I met Herman Kahn. I think it was in the spring of 1983 that I attended an American Association for the Advancement of Science (AAAS) annual meeting in Detroit. Prior to that, I had stumbled across a copy of Kahn's book *The Next 200 Years: A Scenario for America and the World* (Morrow, 1976) that he coauthored with William Brown and Leon Martel, so I knew about Kahn. As one might suspect, *The Next 200 Years* presents an optimistic scenario of economic conditions in the year 2176, because it was Kahn's contention that all of the looming catastrophes can be overcome, including all-out nuclear war.

At the AAAS meeting, Kahn hosted a session and panel discussion with Julian Simon that was entitled something like *The Resourceful Earth: A Response to Global 2000,* which was later crafted into a book of the same name (Blackwell, 1984). Of course, they promoted the sweetness and light view of the future, but eventually acknowledged that there were looming environmental crises that would have to be dealt with. The audience was not so welcoming, especially after Kahn talked about extinctions.

We could not worry about all the animals on the planet, Kahn stated. We should only endeavor to save the really big iconic ones (like whales, eagles, and elephants) and the really cute ones (like pandas). All those other little insignificant ones (many birds, some fish, some plants, tons of insects, etc) we should just let go. I would suspect that he'd have added wolves to the lot (too dangerous to be around humans) and possibly things like bats (too fragile and occasionally rabid) and bears (for the same reason as wolves, but it would be okay if they just stayed in Canada). I am not sure how he would have classified lions and tigers.

I corralled Kahn in the hallway after the meeting and asked him if he wasn't in danger of promoting inactivity by saying the doomsday folks were wrong. If people are convinced the future is going to be rosy, why would they do anything about the coming crises? To Herman Kahn's credit, he did acknowledge that I was right on that point. But he did not change his opinion about the emerging reality, nor did he change his thinking about animals and human-caused extinctions.

So this is my take on Herman Kahn's classification of life forms, which may be what a lot of other people are thinking, too, including many of those in America's Heartland:

1. Stuff you can eat and that you want to keep eating, so you have to give it some protection.
2. Stuff you don't eat and you can let die.
3. Really big animals like the ones you see in zoos; these should be given enough protection to keep the zoos stocked.
4. Really cute animals that your grandkids won't let you kill.
5. Humans (it is okay if lots of them die, especially if you don't know them or they are illegal immigrants).

It would be nice to think the average person doesn't classify life forms that way, but I have to remember that the average person isn't like me. I also have to remember that it was just shortly after the 1983 meeting that Herman Kahn died of a stroke. My guess is he was eating too much red meat.

I'm not sure where deer and raccoons fit into those categories, but I suspect they could be safely in Category 1 (as well as more manageable in number) if we had a good deer/raccoon cookbook. That's probably where I'd want to be if I was on the other side of the human/animal divide, since I don't fall into the "really cute" category. So I want to challenge one of our fine Vashon restaurants to get the ball rolling and offer a venison entrée. Given our growing preference for natural foods, the first restaurant to do it could make a lot of doe.

What deer look like to you.

What deer look like to your plants.

Vashon's History (good bedtime reading)

WHEN I WAS in 8th grade, we were required to take an American history class taught by Miss Ruel. Miss Ruel was an erstwhile and dedicated teacher who knew her subject, but she struggled greatly with the class in which I was a student. "Everyone should know history," she drummed into us, knowing that some students would require more drumming than others. For me in particular, she had more pointed remarks. "If you don't remember history," she told me, "you are doomed to repeat this class." Fortunately, I did not have to repeat that class, but I came close when I got a D on the final.

The irony was that I have always been interested in history, it was just that I didn't do so well in her class. For example, years later when I was in college, I took an elective class on History of the American West, and I got the highest grade in the class. Both the professor and I counted this as quite an accomplishment, because I was the only geology major in the class and the rest of the students were history majors, who understandably were upset with my performance. What I had going for me was that I had already visited most of the places the professor described. I could easily picture Crazy Horse at the Little Big Horn because I had stood on that spot. Given the topography, it was no surprise to me at all that Custer had bitten the big one.

But 8th grade was another matter. I hated studying (I still do) and reasoned that Miss Ruel's final test would not be an accurate assessment of what I had learned unless I purposely did NOT study. For me to cram for the test would be unfair to my teacher because it would not provide a valid assessment of her teaching skills. That's why I got a D. Oddly, she never thanked me for being statistically valid.

My reason for relating this story is to explain why I didn't study for this chapter. Vashon's history is reportedly long and interesting, at least to some, but I just skimmed over the tables of contents of a few books in order to summarize it here. So I have a darn good reason why this section is a little light on actual history. And besides, it's my opinion that a good story is always better than the truth. People remember good stories. History is forgotten by us all the time. Why spend time writing it down if we are going to repeat it?

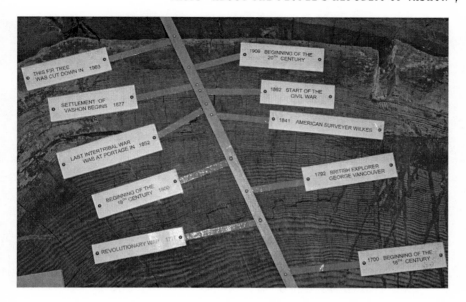

My source for most of the "data" in this section was this display of tree rings in the Vashon-Maury Island Heritage Museum.

I have noticed that history is usually discussed starting at the be-ginning. For the Pacific Northwest, this usually means starting at the end of the Ice Age (Pleistocene, to us geologists). It goes something like this: First, the glaciers melt. Then, animals and plants cover the land again and people arrive. After the first people arrive, then it's just more people of different types arriving later, with each succes-sive wave displacing the preceding one. Some people fight with one another (no surprise there) and some just steal from each other or take their women (again, no surprise). It's both boring and predictable un-til the attorneys show up and then all Hell breaks loose.

Rather than reciting the real history here in more detail, I'd prefer to refer you to the books that I skimmed because they do a much better job anyway (the authors studied) and they easily can be found in the library or local bookstores. One is an annotation and expan-sion of *Van Olinda's History of Vashon-Maury Island* by Roland Carey (Alderbrook Publ. Co., 1985). It is a good source of detailed history for Vashon and also great bedtime reading. Once I found the list of people who served in World War I, it was dreamsville for me.

Probably the most popular book on Vashon history is a beautiful new publication by Bruce Haulman and Jean Cammon Findlay titled simply *Vashon-Maury Island* from the Images of America series by Arcadia Publishing (2011). It is crammed full of great photos and interesting discussion, and it is available at lots of local bookstores. I highly recommend it.

Another of my favorites is *A History of Vashon-Maury Island, Re-addressed*, by Nancy Silver (privately published), available at the History Museum run by the Vashon-Maury Heritage Association, and possibly elsewhere. It's a great walking and windshield guide to 200+ sites, with each described succinctly. You can drive or walk around with this publication in your pocket and check out lots of interesting buildings and historic sites. It contains both Nancy's inside knowledge and aside comments that are thought-provoking and fun. Where she got all this information is beyond me.

Most history books claim that Vashon was discovered by Capt. George Vancouver in 1792, but we all know that Native Americans lived here for thousands of years before that. Sadly, other than for corrupted place names, little evidence of their presence remains. There is a great summary of that history in *Vashon Island Archaeology, A View From Burton Acres Shell Midden*, edited by Julie Stein and Laura Phillips (Univ. of Washington Press, Burke Museum Cultural Research Report No. 8, 2002), available in most local book stores. In that book, you can learn about the various ethnic groups that inhabited this region and discover their unpronounceable names. For example, when I first moved to the Seattle area, I noticed that you could separate long-time residents from newcomers just by listening to the way they pronounced the name of the town of Puyallup. Tukwila is another town name that some folks butcher, and Des Moines is not pronounced the way you might expect.

A very good book on recent Native American history in the Seattle area is *Native Seattle* by Coll Thrush (University of Washington Press,

2007), also available in local book stores. After reading it, all I can say is that it's a good thing for European Americans that the local tribes had no access to modern attorneys when we drained their lakes, killed their salmon, and told them to live someplace else. We'd have all been sued up one side and down the other.

An early ferry (the *Vashon*) now housed in the Vashon-Maury Island Heritage Museum. This particular boat was replaced with a larger version when it was discovered that no actual people could fit in it.

The Muckleshoots are a tribe that still has property on the island (principally for shellfish harvesting) and years ago had ancestors living here. According to *Vashon Island Archaeology*, pre-European residents included the S'Homamish people. Van Olinda also states that another tribe, the Nisquallys, stretched nets at Portage to catch low-flying birds. Somewhere I read (although I can't find the reference now) that the Nisqually and S'Homamish peoples had a resource-sharing arrangement for Portage that allowed both to use the same location for different purposes.

From my extensive review of the literature, it is pretty clear that Vashon's history prior to the white man's invasion is both light on actual data and filtered by Anglo-Saxon indifference. This same pattern has been repeated elsewhere, and seems to be part and parcel of both capitalism and American hegemony. Some famous Presidents, including our current one, have tried to change that, but without much success.

Speaking of famous residents, we've had a few on the islands. Betty MacDonald, author of a number of books including *The Egg And I,* resided here for a while on the north end. Her farm was (and may still be for all I know) a bed and breakfast where you could book a room.

For those of you into TV trivia, John Ratzenberger (who played Cliff Clavin on *Cheers*) lived for a while in a nice home on the east side of Quartermaster Harbor. I once visited this house (when John was not at home) to evaluate a building proposal for the County. John wanted to build a bulkhead on the beach, but the County could not allow it because it did not meet the criteria for an allowed shoreline alteration. John and his wife sold the house and moved back to California shortly thereafter, but I cannot say if his experience with the County led to their decision to move. What I do know is that some people reported that his wife was tired of the long dark winters, and others have said that John got very irritated when islanders called him Cliff in public. According to information I gleaned from a minutes-long internet search, John and his wife divorced a year or two after they moved away from Vashon, suggesting yet a third reason to move: a remedy for marital discord.

If those are not enough reasons to move away from the Pacific Northwest, I can list one more. John Ratzenberger was a strong supporter of conservative causes, and appeared with Kelsey Grammer at several Republican Party events during the 2008 presidential race in support of John McCain. He also was outspoken in opposition to the

2009 health care reform bill, referring to it as socialism. Given island-ers' tendency to side with the Democrats and liberal social causes, I'm guessing that John found himself outnumbered in the political realm.

Speaking of politics, we've also been home to several famous politicians and businessmen. At least two ex-Governors have resided for years near Burton on a street now called "Governor's Row," and Vashon has been a favorite hangout of other influential personalities. For example, Thomas Stewart, chairman and CEO of Services Group of America (a privately held food service corporation that he founded 20 years ago and that currently boasts 4,000 employees and annual sales of more than $2.5 billion), lived here on what is still the island's largest estate, Misty Isle Farm. In 2006, he moved to Arizona citing the Washington Legislature's decision to enact an inheritance tax that would have cost his estate millions had he been a Vashon resident at the time of his death. Ironically, it was just four years after moving to the southwest to avoid the inheritance tax that Stewart and his family were killed in a helicopter accident. Misty Isle Farm was put on the market in 2007 for $125 million, but never sold and was later taken off the market.

In addition to supporting the Vashon equestrian community and fi-nancing the annual July 4th fireworks display in Quartermaster Harbor, Tom Stewart was a staunch Republican who supported his party by holding annual summer picnics at Misty Isle Farm. His picnics were fa-mous for drawing GOP luminaries such as Newt Gingrich, Jack Kemp and Trent Lott. But his salad days in the Republican Party ended in 1998 following a felony conviction for violating federal election laws. According to press reports, Stewart laundered $100,000 in campaign contributions to GOP candidates through his company's employees. Most of that money was directed toward the congressional campaign of his friend and former Vashon neighbor, Pete Von Reichbauer, who is currently a King County councilman. Stewart was ordered to pay $5 million in fines and serve 60 days of house arrest, the third-largest penalty in U.S. history for a violation of that kind.

Another less-controversial Stewart also resides here, at least part-time. Jim Stewart (no relation to Tom), founder of Stewart Brothers Coffee (which later became Seattle's Best Coffee and then was purchased by Starbucks), did a lot of his early company development at the old roasterie on the northwest corner of SW Cemetery Road and Vashon Highway SW. The roasterie is one of the island's most historic buildings (and a must-see) and currently houses another coffee company, The Vashon Island Coffee Roasterie, which shares the building with Minglement, an organic health food and herb store. The roasterie building was the site of Stewart's original coffee shop, The Wet Whisker.

Despite the presence of influential politicians and captains of industry, it is the profusion of artists, musicians, and performers for which Vashon is best known. There are way too many people to list here, but some present (and past) residents' names I can drop include Berkeley Breathed (cartoonist, creator of *Bloom County*, and author of *Red Ranger Came Calling*, which is set on Vashon, and who still has family here), Dan Savage (author, pundit, and journalist best known for *Savage Love*), and Johnny Depp (he has been "sighted" only). I am also proud to report that all island residents are separated from Kevin Bacon by just two degrees, but I won't say why. And other famous (and thought to be deceased) luminaries such as Sonny Bono (in the company of Cher) and Albert Einstein have been sighted at performances of the Church of Great Rain, a local comedy group. If you haven't seen a Church of Great Rain performance, you certainly should.

There is also a wealth of secretive and fictitious authors on Vashon, including such people as Will North (who claims to be writing a new novel), Cecil Benthos (who claims to be a treasure hunter and has written the only catalog of lost mines on Vashon, available in local bookstores), and Victor Bravo Monchego (who claims to have interviewed Donald Rumsfeld). These "gentlemen," and I use that term loosely, and more like them can be found on the internet by simply Googling their names. You will almost certainly find out more than you want to know, but isn't that why history is so fascinating?

I have to take a nap now.

Vashon's Militaristic Foundations (this part is TOP SECRET)

YOU HAVE TO look to see traces of it today, but Vashon was once a bastion in the decades-long war against godless Communism. By that I mean that we were home to a Nike missile base that existed from 1956 until 1974.

Vashon hasn't been the only place in western Washington to benefit from Pentagon budgets. A number of old forts and shoreline defenses were established throughout Puget Sound as early as the 1800s, and some still exist as parks and recreational areas. For example, Admiralty Inlet (near Port Townsend) was considered so strategic to the defense of Puget Sound during the 1890s that three forts (Fort Worden, Fort Flagler, and Fort Casey) were built around the inlet. Their huge guns were oriented to create a "Triangle of Fire" that could thwart any invasion attempt by sea. Why anyone would want to invade Port Townsend is beyond me, unless it was to quash any effort to create a jazz festival. Sadly, no anti-jazz invasion ever materialized.

One of the authors investigating a cannon at Ft. Casey.

Vashon's close association with the military goes back to World War II, when Army units were assigned here as part of the Puget Sound defense system. Beginning in 1942, Army personnel were based on the island, with headquarters at the Center School (southeast corner of Vashon Highway and SW 204th) and volunteer-staffed observation posts at Cove and at Pembroke on Maury Island. In 1943, the Army Fighter Command took charge of monitoring aircraft flying above Vashon, displacing the volunteers, who were doing the best they could.

In 1952, with the advent of the Cold War and the perceived vulnerability of Seattle to atomic attack, another observation post was established on Vashon with 70 trained Civil Defense volunteers. The following year, Anti-Aircraft Battery C ("Charlie Battery") of the 513th Air Defense Battalion was stationed on Vashon where the Eagles Aerie is located today, and presumably the volunteers were once again without a job. Charlie Battery came complete with anti-aircraft guns, but I don't know in which direction they were pointed, unless it was at the volunteers.

In 1956, the Sunrise Ridge administrative site and the Paradise Ridge site were purchased and jointly converted into one of 12 Nike missile sites that surrounded Seattle, known as the Metropolitan Defense Ring. Sunrise Ridge was originally a strawberry farm that at one time was owned and operated by the Matsumoto family, some of whom spent World War II in internment camps.

Battery A of the 433rd Anti-Aircraft Artillery Missile Battalion operated the Nike base from 1956 until it was closed in 1974. There were more than a few Ajax and Hercules launchers there over the years, as well as administration and maintenance buildings and housing. The battery lasted for nearly 20 years. It just kept going, and going.

It is not true, or at least no one will admit, that Vashon residents once aimed this gun at Maury Island. If that were to happen, a strategic target would be Dockton Road just east of Portage, close to the same stretch of road that King County is thinking about removing. Coincidence?

Many of you Baby Boomers probably remember the Cuban Missile Crisis and the dark fears we schoolchildren harbored during the Cold War. I can remember receiving instructions in grade school about what we should do if the Russkies bombed Cincinnati. Clear away from the windows, dive under a desk, and cover your head and face with your arms, was what we were told. We were also directed to a "bomb shelter" in the newest wing of the school (Monfort Heights Elementary), which was really just a basement storage room. There was supposed to be a supply of emergency water (in big drums) along with boxes of crackers in the "bomb shelter." We pestered our teacher incessantly for a taste of the crackers, but she never relented. I think it was because she knew damn well that there were no crackers.

Looking back, it is really sad that kids even as young as five or six were taught to be prepared for instant annihilation. This kind of training is not easily overcome, and I'm sure it allowed more than a few therapists to make their boat payments in future years. I can remember having discussions with my grade school friends (in 1962) as to whether the Russians would bomb the elementary school before they targeted the high school. If they went for the high school only (because those students were closer to being eligible for the military), we were safe. After much thoughtful discussion that included coin flips, we finally decided that their targets in Cincinnati, a town of several hundred thousand people, would include (in this order): first the airport, then the train station, Colerain High School, and finally Monfort Heights Elementary. We resigned ourselves to the idea that there was no way we could avoid a day in the "bomb shelter," but at least there would be crackers.

It was in the early 1990s that I first went to Russia on business. For this child of the Cold War (and a James Bond fan), going into the former Soviet Union was both a treat and a challenge. I saw spies where none existed and none where many existed. I met "former" KGB agents who had become "businessmen" and naïve (but likeable) local administrators who did not begin to understand the fundamentals of capitalism. I learned that the Russian word for computer is komputer and that the Russian word for profit doesn't exist. I also learned that almost nothing worked in Russia. "We were afraid of the Russians??" I asked myself. "They can't even get their phones to work! How could they have possibly found their way to Monfort Heights Elementary?!?"

In 1976, well before the Cold War officially ended, the Vashon Nike base was decommissioned. The missile silos at Paradise Ridge were filled and Sunrise Ridge was quitclaimed to the Vashon-Maury Health Services Center, which converted one of the buildings into a health clinic that is still in operation. Sunrise Ridge is also home to the food bank, Granny's Attic (a thrift store), Voice of Vashon radio and two sports fields. Paradise Ridge was similarly decommissioned and given to King County, who tried to give it back in 1983. This action by the County prompted a group of islanders to mobilize and create what became the Vashon Park District, of which Paradise Ridge Equestrian Park is now a part.

Reports that there are buried warheads at both Sunrise Ridge and Paradise Ridge are probably not accurate, but despite a minutes-long internet search, this author has not been able to determine where the missiles were taken. Just to be on the safe side, you might want to step gingerly if you visit those places. Avoid kicking anything that looks like a nosecone.

Governance (such as it is)

GOVERNANCE OF THE islands should be such a dull topic that you'd be inclined to skip this section. Instead, on Vashon it's a topic of spirited discussion at every coffee stand and wherever else our politically involved populace decides to meet up. Arguments about the nature and relevance of governance are often the only things to read in the island papers (*The Beachcomber*, and our emergency backup paper, *The Loop*) that don't induce heavy eyelids.

Even though it looks like there's a town out here, all parts of both islands are in unincorporated King County. This means that we are regulated by King County codes and serviced by county agencies, including the Seattle & King County Department of Public Health, the Department of Development and Environmental Services, the King County Sheriff, etc. There is more than a little controversy about that, and some people oppose county regulations with the same intensity that they would if they were battling Darth Vader's Empire. A few of these people show up with protest signs at public meetings from time to time, usually getting their facts wrong and accidentally lopping off limbs with their light sabers. But I think it is safe to say that most islanders either don't think about it or are reasonably happy with King County, at least until they apply for a building permit.

Of course, there are also State regulations to address when it comes to construction and land development near the marine shoreline. Things can get pretty complex when it comes time to replace your bulkhead. It is for this reason that I prefer living on top of a hill (with a great view) rather than on the beach (with all the dead smelly things and 96% of the rat population). Not to say that life in a beach cabin with the rats and the dead things isn't idyllic...it just isn't for me.

Even though we have no actual government on Vashon that isn't imposed from outside, we do have an Unofficial Mayor and currently we have a Community Council. Neither has any substantive authority, but both provide hours of amusement for our generally quiet community.

The Unofficial Mayor is elected every year from candidates who campaign as supporters of their favorite charity, and the candidates do not have to be actual human beings. Votes are counted as one for each dollar contributed for that charity in the name of the candidate. Usually, there are two or three people vying for the position (sometimes with a dog or a ferret), often campaigning by holding up traffic and asking for donations. Of course, there is no election commission watching this process, so any candidate could buy the election at the last minute. I'm convinced this happened at least once during my time here. But the great thing about buying this election is that it doesn't matter at all. More money goes to the charities and the "elected" official has no authority and no responsibilities. In fact, after the election, it's likely you'll forget who won the post, or even see them until the following year when they might try to run for re-election by stuffing dollar bills into the ballot box. I view this as a perfect blend of capitalism, democracy, and philanthropy. Except for the philanthropy, it's just like national politics.

The Community Council is a little different. Officially called the Vashon-Maury Island Community Council, the Council is composed of all Island residents aged 18 and over, whether they know it or not. Monthly General Meetings are held in a town hall-style forum. Basically, whoever shows up at the General Meetings gets to discuss and decide whatever there is to discuss and decide. Decisions are made by a public vote at the General Meetings. Much of the work of the Council takes place in the Committees, which then forward their recommendations to the whole Council for action. There is usually not much "action" in action.

Until recently, our Council was recognized by King County as an Unincorporated Area Council (or UAC), meaning that it received support from King County in order to facilitate operations and interaction with County agencies. Along with this designation came a certain amount of respect, but the Council itself had no regulatory authority. Rather, the Council advised County agencies and personnel on relevant topics and acted as a lobbyist for the community. The Council's UAC status, however, was eliminated when the King County Council voted to do away with the UACs and instead have "community service areas," which require no funding and probably not much else either. As of this writing, the community service areas haven't quite been established, or maybe they have and we haven't yet been given the news that we are to be grouped with Black Diamond.

The Council as it stands is led by nine Board members who are elected for set terms. Normally this system has worked pretty well, but in the late summer of 2010, one rather opinionated Council member (of whom there are several, but this one I'll call "Mr. B") made an issue of public accountability and transparency. Lawsuits were threatened. In the end, all nine Board members resigned within the week, although thankfully one (the person who had authority to sign checks) came back to comprise a one-person Board until elections could be held.

You should know that Mr. B had a history of lawsuits. Not long before this event, he had sued King County and the Community Council Board for allowing what he claimed was an under-the-table rezone of the largest industrial parcel on the island (the old K2 Sports plant). The rezoning allowed both residential and retail development where none had been allowed before. I seem to recall that the lawsuit failed because he was not judged to have "standing," meaning it was no skin off of Mr. B's nose if the property was rezoned, so he had no right to complain. Whether the rezone was done improperly was not formally addressed.

You should also know that I like and admire Mr. B. He is one of the island's visionaries, he's always interesting to talk to, and he would give you the shirt off his back, even without the threat of a lawsuit.

So the unlikely resignation of the entire Board (minus one) had many of us both terribly frustrated and enormously humored. The first General Meeting after the mass resignations was probably the best attended meeting in years, and I am guessing that more than a few folks were there just for the spectacle. About 80 people attended, some clearly about to explode with comments and others providing supportive applause and stern looks. This was small-town politics at its finest. Unfortunately, the meeting immediately bogged down because of limitations in either the Bylaws or *Robert's Rules of Order*. A lot of us were still wondering what caused the Board to implode, and several were ready to assign blame for the disaster. It seemed as if roughly three-quarters of that meeting was devoted to deciding if the Board still existed, ever existed, or simply needed a time-out in the corner. At one point, I was convinced that the Board had been abducted by aliens. In the end, we accepted their resignations even though the resignations, and our acceptance of them, may have been unlawful according to the Bylaws.

Which brings me to another point. It is clear that one crank armed with Bylaws and *Robert's Rule of Order* can precipitate the downfall of Western Civilization. Forget about nuclear weapons; my recommendation is to ban Robert's Rules before you get tied up with a mess of motions and can't remember which have been seconded.

However, we did not recognize that problem until after motions started flying around the room like moths around a street light. One proposed to tell King County to stuff it, which I thought was a big mistake. Others made more sense, but no one made the motion I was thinking of making, which was to create a "Tire Pressure Committee" that would monitor discussions at every Council meeting and identify people who mentioned the words "lawsuit" or "public information request." After each meeting, the TP Committee could convene in the parking lot and let the air out of all four tires of the offenders' cars. Public discourse might become a little more congenial after that.

Wife Margaret and granddaughter Sophie posing with one of the recent candidates for Community Council Board.

Toward the end, it became clear that there were several options: 1) stay the same with new or recycled board members (turnover is great and the gene pool is tiny), 2) create an "enhanced" Community Council (super-charged is the term I prefer) that still had connections to King County, 3) drop out of the UAC system (we were later kicked out anyway), or 4) do something really creative like forming a new county, township, or city, even though none of these options were thought to be legal.

If you know anything about politics, you can guess what happened next: not much. A new Board was elected and they proceeded to bicker about what to do. I went to several of these meetings, and I remember that we considered lots of alternatives, but we quickly ruled out oligarchies, monarchies, social democracies, fascist dictators, and Soviet-style collectives. I was up for returning to our roots, which is being tribal hunter-gatherers, and my wife thought we should elect our Board members by having a dance competition. I can polka pretty well, so under her system I could get elected even though I'm a County employee.

Just when we were thinking the fun was over, another opinionated islander (Ms. C) presented a motion to the Council to have Mr. B (who had been elected to the new Board) thrown out. The next general meeting (at which this motion was to be voted upon) drew an even larger crowd. Impassioned testimony was given denouncing Mr. B, but a super majority was needed to vote him out and the motion failed by just a few votes.

Rumors circulated later that just prior to the meeting, one Board member had rounded up a bunch of bar patrons and other folks of the type who don't attend Council meetings, and got them to vote following her signals. If it really happened, it may have been that action that allowed Mr. B to retain his seat.

Now, if you're like me, you might question the ethics of the bar-hopping Board member. Or you might just decide that you're sick and tired of all the fuss and you'd like to end it all. Some folks who appear to have had this idea started a competing group called the "All-Island Forum" that is designed to be more free-wheeling and responsive to islanders needs, which may mean that they get even less done. We'll see, because the Forum has just gotten started, but it may very well be the first step towards declaring independence from King County and from Washington State!

If you are this goofy...I mean, if you think this is a good idea, you're in luck because one of the art galleries on the island held a competition to design a flag for Vashon, and we now have an official flag! With a flag, we can have an army, with uniforms (purple loosely fitted ones made of hemp) and cool patches that say things like "V is for Vashon." We can give ourselves titles (dibs on "Great Grand Lizard") and offer discounts at local stores for Vashon Liberation Army inductees. If the store owners don't agree, we can declare martial law and set our own prices for beer! We can outlaw lighted signs (even existing ones), establish our own marijuana policy, and let local hunters "control" the deer population from their back porches. We can declare an Official State Fossil (elected yearly from local politicians and businessmen) and an Official State

Religion (Waffling). All of this will be really easy once we figure out how to pay for everything.

So I invite you all to join this effort by throwing your hat in the ring, raising your hand, and jumping on board, not necessarily at the same time. With your help, Vashon independence finally will be achieved, unless King County expels us first.

The "official" flag of Vashon; see color version on the front cover
(image courtesy of the designer, Adria Magrath).

Getting Around and Away (as fast as possible)

IN CASE YOU hadn't noticed, Vashon is surrounded by water. This fact sometimes makes it rather challenging to travel from where you are to where you want to go. Not that Americans are inexperienced with travel complications. Due solely to the size of America, to get from one place to another typically requires the assistance of a gasoline-powered engine, and so Americans have become slaves to their automobiles. On Vashon, we are also slaves to the Washington State Ferry System.

There are two ferry docks on the island, one on the north end and one on the south end. The south-end ferry connects to Tacoma. From the north-end dock, you can travel to Fauntleroy in West Seattle or west to Southworth. There is also passenger-only passage on weekdays from the north-end dock directly to downtown Seattle, and vice versa.

If you are thinking of moving here and working in Seattle, you might want to give it more consideration before selling your house on the mainland. For the commuter, life is all about the ferry schedule. From the time you leave the house until the moment you return, your entire day is set by the ferry schedule, as is your night in preparation for the next day. The commutes are typically long and complicated, but with experience, you can shave off travel times by knowing exactly when to get in line to board the next boat. Each sailing has a set number of cars it can accommodate, so you have to figure out where in line you have to be to make your sailing. If you get in line just a little late, plan on waiting for the next boat. I can tell you from personal experience that it is extremely frustrating to have gotten in line too far back by one car length. Even without missed-boat delays, one-way commutes from Vashon to Seattle, depending upon where you work and live, can be 90 minutes long. The good thing is that you will be sitting in your parked car or on the ferry for much of that time, and you can catch up on your reading or your sleep.

I have discovered, however, that sleeping is not something all of us should do while waiting in a ferry line or during the ferry crossing. Unless you are a very light sleeper, you could be rudely aroused from your slumber by either a crescendo of honking horns or a ferry worker pounding on your windshield. Either way, it's no treat, especially if you have your big dog in the car (as I usually do) who does not take kindly to strangers pounding on the windshield.

If you can, it's much better to park your car and ride across as a foot passenger. You just have to be there on time to make the sailing because there is no need to wait in a line. You also get to load and unload first, but of course there is no car for you on the other side. Unless you have arranged other transportation, you'll have to take the Metro bus, which is not an unpleasant experience and is reasonably priced. There is even Metro bus service on Vashon going from one end of the island to the other, and to Dockton on Maury Island. Unfortunately, the time between runs can be long, and there is no service at all on Sundays.

Speaking of foot traffic, let's not forget what we used to call the Passenger Only Ferry, now known as the King County Water Taxi. This is a passenger-only boat that runs just a few times in the mornings and evenings on weekdays (for downtown Seattle commuters) from the north-end dock directly to downtown Seattle and back. It's a lot of fun to ride and very reasonably priced, but the travel times are quite restricted. You can take your bike with you, but leave the big dog at home. I understand the Water Taxi is haunted, but I have no evidence of same.

Speaking of bikes, Vashon is known far and wide as a haven for Spandex-clad cyclists. There are few actual bike lanes out here, and those that exist are not very wide, but traffic is minimal compared to Seattle so there is a reasonably good chance that you won't end up as a hood ornament. Well...less than 20% chance anyway.

Local transportation can be by either boat or automobile...or in this case, both.

If you can't ride a bike (presumably for medical reasons or because you're allergic to Spandex), you can actually fly into Vashon via a small plane. Of course, you'll have to rent one because there is no regularly scheduled commercial service. I had the pleasant experience last year of being a passenger on the short flight of a small plane (it took a crowbar to get me out of the back seat) that left Vashon's airport, flew around Mt. Rainier (to examine the glaciers), and then returned to Vashon's airport. It was a fun trip. Given the short approach distance at the Vashon airport and numerous nearby trees, I will forever be grateful for the excellent flying skills of the pilot, George Kirkish, who operates both a flying service and one of Vashon's fine wineries. Sadly, we were not served any of his wine during the flight, but it's possible that when he sees this in print, he may hire a stewardess. She should be equipped with both a corkscrew and a crowbar.

Giving a thumbs-up to George's flying reminds me to talk about thumbing. Yes, I am actually referring to that action that probably was banned by your parents because they taught you that the roads are rife with serial killers and sexual deviants who are driving around hoping to pick up someone looking for a ride. Stick out your thumb and find the path to your grave, was the image left with me as a child in Ohio. Then again, I was also told that if I ate raw cookie dough, it would make a big indigestible ball in my stomach. My grandmother told me this, and I suspect it was because she wanted the Toll House cookie dough as much as I did.

It's true that in Ohio, sexual predators and serial killers may be an issue, but here on Vashon there are fewer characters of this type. As a result, thumbing a ride has actually become somewhat of an art form for many teenagers and a few older slackers. Only a few have experienced problems to date, mostly in the form of stolen homework papers, or so they have claimed to their teachers. Sadly, I do not expect our thumb-friendly environment to survive forever given the onslaught of "culture" from across the water.

A typical morning view of the Southworth-Vashon-Fauntleroy ferry when it's not raining. I think those are mountains in the background, but I see them so infrequently that I'm not sure.

Which brings us back to the ferries. There are two important rules you need to remember about riding the Washington State Ferry System: 1) Never lock your car if you have a car alarm, and 2) Never EVER cut into line. The first rule you can use to separate islanders from tourists. Tourists always lock their car and head up to the passenger deck, forgetting that the boat rocks a bit. But no need to worry because they are quickly notified over the loud speaker to please go back to their car and disable the alarm. The second rule is so important that it recently became a state law, but even before it became a state law, it was an important rule of ferry etiquette.

As an example, my charming wife once accidentally cut into a ferry line of cars that were waiting to board at the north end. We live on the north end, and for north-enders in our neighborhood, the approach to the dock is east on 112th to Vashon Highway, and then left on the highway. The problem is that the 112th/Highway intersection is often in the middle of a line of waiting traffic. If the line begins to move, and some knucklehead who has fallen asleep up the hill does not wake up soon enough, a large gap forms that looks very much like the end of the line. So when Margaret pulled up to the intersection, she thought she was merging into traffic rather than cutting into line.

Margaret had two of her three kids in the car, and she was taking them to the airport for a holiday visit with their dad. She was rather stressed about it all because the travel schedule was tight and her ex-husband was involved. That alone should be sufficient to explain her subsequent actions.

The line closed up and inched down the hill to the ferry dock, where it stopped because the boat that was loading then had filled. She was caught between cars in front and behind and a second line to her left that prevented her from pulling out of line even if she wanted to. But Margaret didn't know she was in a predicament until the driver immediately behind her knocked on her window and informed her that she had cut in line. I presume this was the guy who had fallen asleep, and to his credit he was polite enough. She replied that she was sorry, she didn't know, and left it at that. A few minutes later, another courteous islander knocked on her window and asked her if she knew she had cut in line. "Yes...I know...it was an accident," she said, with mounting frustration. Moments later, a third "courteous" islander knocked on her window and was not so understanding. He was needlessly frank about his opinion of her actions and informed her that he was telling the state trooper at the end of the dock, which he promptly did.

The next boat began to load. When Margaret's car reached the trooper, a large man who clearly lacked a sense of humor, he motioned for her to pull out of line and wait in the parking area. This meant that Margaret would miss the boat she had planned to catch, and all because of a mistake that one could argue was started by the guy who fell asleep and had already boarded the boat.

The trooper came up to her window and demanded to know why she had cut in line. Margaret replied that she didn't cut in line, it was a mistake, and she was sorry. Unfortunately, the trooper did not take the time to ask Margaret how it could have been a mistake. Instead, he accused her of lying.

Margaret's next action was one that to this day makes me smile and incredibly proud to be married to such a spunky person. She calmly looked him straight in the eye and told this towering, red-faced, uniformed and gun-toting state trooper to "F—k off."

The trooper was momentarily flustered, but he recovered and threatened to fine her $100 just for that remark. "I'm a professional!" he screamed, oblivious to the irony, "I don't deserve such treatment!" There was no state law about cutting into line at that time, so there would have been no ticket written for that part of it; the ticket he promised was only for the F-word comment. The trooper took her driver's license and stomped back to the office to write the ticket. At that point, Margaret called me and asked for some assistance.

I rushed down the hill and parked next to Margaret's van. The trooper was in the office fuming about such unprofessional behavior as was exhibited by my wife, and I introduced myself. He yelled at me for a bit as well, but I empathized with his plight and explained that I understood his frustration with the public because I also worked for the government. I went on to explain that folks who live on the north end typically get into the ferry line from 112th, and what can happen if someone is pokey farther up the hill.

A few minutes later, I walked up to Margaret, who was calmly sitting in her car with the kids, and handed her the driver's license. "There won't be any fine," I told her, "I took care of things." She was thankful and questioned how I managed that, but she was glad the experience was over. Fortunately, she was able to board the next boat in time to get her kids to the airport, and I was there to experience her resilience in the face of an unfair challenge from authority. I also learned that I had better never cross this gal, and neither should you. Vashon women are not to be messed with.

Food (which restaurant went out of business this week?)

NOT LONG AGO, I was on a mission regarding our restaurants. I presented to several people, including the editor of a local paper, the idea that we should have a restaurant critic on Vashon. I could be that critic, I told them. I could get free meals (paid for by the paper) and ruthlessly critique bland cuisine while cloaked in anonymity (I would use a pen name). Maybe the food would improve and the wine servings get bigger!!

I didn't understand until later why they all looked at me as if I had asked them to hold an electric eel. It turns out that in small towns, the reputations of businesses are sacred. One can never ever disparage a business or a businessman, not even when he is convicted of trafficking cocaine. "Sure, he's a drug king-pin," they'd say, "but he's really good at being an attorney!"

If I had thought it through, I'd have figured this out and realized that my restaurant critique idea was naïve at best. Looking back, I'm a little surprised I didn't realize that sooner, because I had lots of experience with small town restaurants (and reputations) from my college days.

When I was a senior at the University of Missouri-Rolla, there was a four-month period when I had dinner most nights at Carter's Café in downtown Rolla, which is nestled in the northern Ozarks of south-central Missouri. In 1974, Carter's Café was a down-home, regular-food restaurant in a humble storefront on the main drag. The most notable thing about the place was their red neon sign. They served standard greasy-spoon fare such as chicken-fried steak, roast chicken and mashed potatoes, fried ham, spaghetti with meat balls, and Salisbury steak, with featured entrees appearing on the same day every week. If nothing else, they were dependable. There was always processed turkey roll and canned cranberry sauce around the holidays, including the fourth of July. It was just like going home, except without the requirement to clean up after yourself.

After a couple of months, I became friends with one of the waitresses who occasionally offered me advice from her mature and worldly position of being married and two years older. Being only 22 years old myself, I was not experienced enough to recognize the flaws in her wisdom.

One Friday evening, I was scheduled to go on a blind date. A friend of a friend of mine had set me up with his girlfriend's girl friend, mainly so that he could get his girlfriend alone. I knew none of these people very well, but I did know that I was nervous, and I showed up to meet the girl without having eaten any dinner. It turned out that they had already eaten, so I excused myself, promising to return in an hour after I had gotten something to eat. They didn't think they'd see me again, but I have always been a man of my word.

I made a beeline for Carter's, ordered the Salisbury steak, and asked my waitress friend what I should do. I didn't like the looks of this girl, I told her, and I was nervous about what they were planning (going to a dance), and I gave her several other excuses that in retrospect said a lot about me and little about my prospective date. My waitress gave me what must be time-tested and universal advice for how to deal with a blind date situation: "Get drunk first."

At the liquor store, I bought a pint of cheap whiskey (I was not a discriminating drinker in those days) and downed half of it in the car. The rest of the evening went a little better. I remember attending a rock music dance in a darkened barn (we actually had dances in barns) and being asked to dance by my blind date. I responded that I did not dance, ever, even though dancing to that kind of music mostly meant jumping around and waving your arms. You could imitate a chimpanzee running in place and get by. Oddly, she accepted my refusal without complaint and dutifully sat next to me for the rest of our time there. I had no clue how generous an act that was.

It was shortly after that weekend that I stopped eating at Carter's Café. No matter how homey the atmosphere, I could not continue going there after finding the second fly in my food. The first was mixed in with the mashed potatoes. The second was perfectly preserved in the middle of a lime Jello cube.

I could not complain widely about Carter's because they were so loved by the townies, but I did complain to my roommate who instantly stopped eating there. I discovered that word-of-mouth is the only effective way to critique restaurants in a small town.

But Carter's did experience a minor downturn in business a few months later when the owner was indicted on Federal racketeering charges, whatever those are. I am thinking the downturn in business was because his accountant, attorney, and investment planner no longer ventured to take their families to the café for dinner. Most people kept eating there, possibly so they could get a good look at a racketeer, who are not especially common in the Missouri Ozarks. Some hard-of-hearing folks might have shown up to see a raconteur or a rocketeer. Aren't Federal rocketeers the same as astronauts?

A number of Vashon farms provide local produce and meats that are both delicious and good for you (photo courtesy of Chip Wright).

You never know what people are thinking in small-town restaurants. The summer of 1973, I was working with three other college students on a geophysical survey outside Boss, Missouri, which even by Ozark standards is a small town. After eating dinner for four nights in a row in the only restaurant around, the waitress (who was all of 16) approached us and said everyone else in the restaurant thought we were members of the St. Louis Cardinals baseball team. I'm not sure where they got that, but we laughed and told her it was not true. In reality, we said, we were pro bowlers on tour. They believed that for another week until someone saw us running survey lines through the woods north of town. The town folks weren't nearly as friendly after that. Even so, at the end of the summer, the waitress wanted to run off with one of my co-workers. Perhaps she still harbored dreams of being a sports figure's wife.

And so here we are on Vashon. We have a number of restaurants, all of which I would classify as exceptional. In truth, when a new restaurant opens, most of the residents just wish that whatever they serve is edible, and we get that wish much of the time.

There is a lot of turnover in restaurants, as you might expect. For example, during the time I have resided on Vashon, I have seen five different restaurants occupy the same space. Some went out of business because it was their personal choice, and some because they could not get enough clients. This is not unusual even for Seattle; the restaurant business is cut-throat and operates on a low profit margin.

So, if you are looking for an enlightened discussion of the varied and flavorful cuisine of Vashon, you had probably better look someplace else. But if you are looking for short quirky remarks on at least some of the food sources on the island, they are immediately below. Some or perhaps all of these restaurants may be closed by the time you get through this chapter. They are not listed in order of importance:

1. **The Hardware Store** – This is actually a restaurant. Thankfully, our real hardware store is not called "The Restaurant," or we'd be eating the wrong kind of nuts. Go if you want a "great good" meal.

2. **Giuseppe's** and/or The Monkey Tree – Now housing Giuseppe's, this restaurant was previously the site of The Monkey Tree (no longer in business), which is described here because of its regional reputation and interesting name. The Monkey Tree was named for a large Monkey Puzzle tree that no longer exists because the neighbor cut it down. A memorial service for the tree was held, but no one suggested planting another tree. The Monkey Tree routinely received glowing reviews in even the Seattle press, but excellent food and a loyal customer base could not prevent its closing. It was our only vegetarian restaurant. When it was open, I'd advise people to take along an extra pair of oversized pants to wear after chowing down on Chef Adam Cone's delicious pastries. After The Monkey Tree closed, Vashonites lost on average 15 pounds each. The building was vacant for a while, and then the business was sold to a new bunch who opened an Italian restaurant called Giuseppe's (which is operating today). Fortunately, Adam is still associated with the restaurant, so there's a chance we'll be able to fit into our XXL slacks once again. And I understand the Italian food is good, too.

3. **Express Cuisine** – Everything is really really good, but my favorite is the stroganoff. Seating is family style (everyone at big tables) so you might have to sit next to someone you don't know. Just order another glass of wine and get over it. Or you could do like me and down half a pint of cheap whiskey in the car before you order your meal.

4. **The Rock** – Our iconic pizza joint. Say hi to Chuck and Carol if they haven't yet spun their last pizza crust and moved to a tropical paradise. They are the most generous wine servers on the island, and the pizza is great, too.

5. **The "Q"** (Quartermaster Inn) in Burton – I didn't know there was a restaurant there for the first three years I lived on Vashon. I have only eaten there once, but if you're near Burton, you should try it. It has been reported that their "small plates are surprisingly

affordable for such a fancy-looking place." I assume the small plates come with food, but I cannot say from experience.

6. **Vashon Tea Shop** – You may be surprised to learn they specialize in tea. They also have pastries, some other good stuff, and miso soup, which looks a lot like tea.

7. **Zoomies** – If you have youngsters, there's no way you can avoid Zoomies, but the burgers are pretty good and so is the ice cream. If it looks like an old Dairy Queen from the outside, that's because it is.

8. **Uptown Takeout** – A family-run restaurant with a few seats for those too tired to return home carrying a meal. Their menu changes daily. What it changes into I cannot say.

9. **Perry's Vashon Burgers** – Another local icon with good eats. I think the flavor of Perry's burgers reminds me a little of White Castle, or as we called them when I was growing up in Cincinnati: Whitey Casstel's. When you live in Cincinnati, you crave the exotic.

10. **Pure** – Speaking of exotic, Pure is an organic juice bar and café serving things like kale, which I would not recognize if I fell into a vat of it. They claim to use "no mysterious ingredients," yet their menu lists "arugula," which must have been named after a first-century Roman Emperor.

11. **Green Ginger Chinese Restaurant** – I am a fan of the mu shu vegetables. When my wife the vegetarian isn't looking, I order the Mongolian beef. In the phone book advertisement, their claim to fame is "NO MSG!" You gotta love these guys.

12. The two island Mexican restaurants – I keep getting their names mixed up, but one is **Casa Bonita** and the other is **La Playa**. One is at the north-end ferry dock and the other is in town. One of them has tasty spinach dishes and the other has good enchiladas. (Whenever I go into a Mexican restaurant, I wonder how much Spanish rice gets thrown away.)

13. **Vashon Eagles #3144** – I'm guessing that your typical world traveler would not be inclined to seek sustenance at an Eagles club.

Nevertheless, it is open to the public for dinner on weeknights, lunch on Thursday, and breakfast on Sunday. I had a meal there once courtesy of the Kiwanis Club and it was so good that I had to let my belt out. Don't worry about the Eagles who hang out there; they won't swoop down on you.

14. Heather's Homegrown Café, soon to be a new Thai restaurant called **May's Kitchen and Bar** – This location in the middle of town was also known as Vashon Homegrown. It used to be Fred's Homegrown before Heather bought it, but that doesn't matter now because Homegrown closed some time back. Recently it was announced that a Thai restaurant will be opening there that will be run by the same person who founded **May**, an exotic Thai restaurant in Wallingford that serves delicious food. Separated as we have been from good Thai food by two miles of water, most Vashonites would kill for a decent green curry. I'm sure the place will be packed when it opens, which will probably be before you read this. Go and try it.

15. **The Red Bicycle Bistro** and **Sporty's** – See the chapter on *Watering Holes*.

16. **The Indian Restaurant now known as Nirvana** – In the very center of town occupying the same space as two previous Indian restaurants (the last of which was known as Spice Route) and at least two restaurants before that (Ferrara and the Stray Dog). I haven't yet eaten at Nirvana because it just opened, but Spice Route's naan alone was worth the price of a meal. You should try Nirvana if it's still there when you read this.

17. **Subway** – I hesitated including Subway here because I could be attacked and beaten with a loaf of French bread by any number of franchise-hating islanders, including my wife. Subway is our only fast food franchise, and likely will remain the only one for a very long time. I have never eaten there (I almost capitalized that so my wife would be sure to see it), but I am guessing it's pretty much like every other Subway. When I need to lose 500 pounds, I may stop by.

18. **La Boucherie** – This is a delightful intimate venue with candle-light and romantic settings in a butcher shop. It is run by one of our island's farms (see below), and features their excellent locally raised meat. Their farmyard is just down the street from where we live, and I walk the dog (Bubby) past there most days. My wife won't eat at La Boucherie because she is a vegetarian and has personally met some of the cutlets. But that doesn't mean you shouldn't.

19. **Bob's Bakery** – No longer run by Bob, but still an excellent bakery. They also offer lunches. Ask them if they have any good Bob stories, and then report back.

20. **Café Luna** – Lots of good coffee drinks, breakfast sandwiches, quiche, teas, lunches, and desserts. If you don't have one of the brownies, you've missed one of life's great pleasures. And they have music every weekend! Go for the funky-mongrel-folk-pop-rock-indy-acoustic-soulful blues. There are too many such musicians to list here.

21. **Sound Food** – This used to be the quintessential Vashon restaurant and funky hangout. The last owners to run a full-time restaurant there got involved with the ferry system, threw up their hands, and left. Now, it is opened occasionally by new tenants who are also caterers. I think it would be a great place to cater a séance. There must be lots of ghosts there.

22. **Gusto Girls** – Speaking of ghosts, my favorite restaurant was Gusto Girls, which is no longer in business. I once danced in a cage in Gusto Girls (just so you don't get the wrong idea, it was the polka), and thankfully nobody had a camera. Gusto Girls occupied the same space as Express Cuisine does today, and reportedly was haunted. I heard about the ghost, an older gentleman spirit, one night at the bar from the proprietor who saw him frequently, but he was seen by others as well. Perhaps he has taken up residence at Express Cuisine, but I've asked twice now and both times was told he wasn't there. Maybe they just don't want to perpetuate any crazy rumors.

23. Grazing at **Thriftway** – Grazing in the grocery store is a favorite past-time of many. There is a good deli section, with soups and salads. You also can eat stuff while you are waiting to pay for it. More than once I've seen a teenager hand an empty bread bag to the checkout clerk for scanning. Try not to get crumbs on the cash register.

24. Grazing in the **Great Outdoors** – There are several experts on edible wild foods on the island, and one writes a column that appears often in the paper. If you are going to eat stuff outdoors, it's better to learn to identify edible things beforehand rather than to rely on trial and error. I suggest you develop a taste for venison and help clean up the dead deer that are so common on the highway. Around here, the automobile is their only natural predator.

25. And lastly, **the farms** – There are a number of wonderful farms that sell local produce in roadside stands, many of which are set up for sales on the "honor method," meaning there's a pile of food and a money can, and it's your job to take what you want and leave the appropriate payment in cash. Some folks have not been very honorable about this. Amazing, isn't it?

Grazing here can be fun. This is the *true* center of the island.

Parking is at a premium in the Vashon town core.

Watering Holes (firewatering holes, rather)

BEING ISLANDS IN Puget Sound, Vashon and Maury are awash in salt water and bilge water. Being in western Washington, we are awash in rainwater as well. Sadly (or happily, depending upon your viewpoint), some folks say we are also awash in alcohol.

There is a state liquor store on the island for those times when you who are looking for cheap whiskey. I've long since outgrown that and moved on to cheap wine and beer, but I did stand in line there once to get a bottle of brandy for the holiday fruitcake. I nearly passed out from the fumes, and that was just from the guy standing in front of me.

Most of the restaurants serve alcohol (how else could they make money?), and at one time there were two that had dueling wine selections: The Hardware Store and Ferrara. Ferrara was a posh Italian restaurant that was located where the Indian restaurant now known as Nirvana is currently, and I remember their wine list as having single bottles that cost as much as $1200. I wish now that I had asked for an empty bottle of $1200 wine, because I'd have refilled it with two-buck Chuck and used it to test the discriminating taste buds of the wine snobs I know.

Sadly, Ferrara closed some time ago, leaving The Hardware Store as the only "destination" wine bar on the island. I've never actually tested The Hardware Store's wine selection, principally because I can't tell most wines apart, but I've heard it's rather noisy in there and not as cheap as the typical Vashon drinker would prefer. By "typical

Vashon drinker" I mean someone you're likely to stand behind in line at the liquor store.

It is true that across America these days, wine is ubiquitous, and we are no less cursed on Vashon. Naïve domestic vintages are for sale just about everywhere except the Public Library. Not long ago there were even two dedicated wine shops on the island with large and esoteric selections that seemed to prosper alongside the two grocery wine departments, and this was for a population of only 11,000 people. That situation didn't last too long, and both wine shops closed. About the time that they closed, Thriftway remodeled and expanded their wine department, almost making up for the loss of both.

We also manufacture wine here. By my count, there are four wineries on the island, all of which turn out significant quantities of premium product. At least one winery occasionally produces a locally grown vintage (there are a few small vineyards on Vashon), but most Vashon wine is made from Columbia Valley grapes. I do not know who does the crushing, but I prefer to imagine it being done by scantily clad young women using the old-fashioned method. Why some vintner hasn't designed a label showing crushing being done that way is totally beyond me, but if someone does, put me down for a case.

As for drinking establishments, several of the restaurants have actual bars, but there are only two classic taverns. The largest tavern, in terms of square footage, is The Red Bicycle Bistro. "The Bike" used to be called Bishop's, probably because the people who owned it were named Bishop. The Bike is divided into two parts: one part that has pool tables and looks like a tavern, and another part that looks like a restaurant and in which there is a stage. They also serve food and specialize in sushi.

I'm not a big fan of sushi because I understand it's made of unusual marine organisms that are not cooked and that are very much like (or identical to) the ones you can touch in the tidal pool exhibit at the Seattle Aquarium. A warning to those who don't know: "Sea Cucumber" contains no actual cucumber, and "calamari" is a fancy name for tentacles with suckers. If that doesn't put you off sushi, I don't know what will.

The Bike is also a favorite venue for musicians, mostly on Friday and Saturday nights. There are some pretty good acts booked there, and some of the shows get positively rowdy. My wife will occasionally drag me there to dance, which I can do really well after I've had a beer or two. Her one complaint is that they don't book any polka bands.

One of the prime ingredients of sushi.

Our other tavern is The Sportsman's Inn, now known as Sporty's, which is conveniently located across the street from The Bike in case you get thrown out of one or the other. Their sign is readable now, but a few years ago the front of the building was graced with something that from a distance looked like this: IPORTIMANI, because the S curves were so shallow that they were practically straight lines.

When I was courting Margaret, we stopped for lunch at The Bike one day and she looked across the street and asked what they sold in Iportimani. My puzzled look came as a surprise to her, and when I figured it out she was terribly embarrassed. We have referred to Sporty's as Iportimani ever since.

I've never had a drink in Iportimani, but I have been there twice for breakfast. Their breakfasts are widely praised, especially the pancakes, and I can confirm that they are to-die-for. There is also a great mural inside that you should see.

Lest you think we are all alcoholics, you should know that there have been, and still are, a number of teetotalers on the island, including one who ran for President twice on the Prohibition ticket.

Gene Amondson was an island icon who raged against the prevalence of alcohol until his untimely death in 2009. A Methodist preacher by training, Gene delivered anti-alcohol speeches across the nation and in some foreign countries, and was often photographed wearing a Grim Reaper outfit in front of wineries or breweries. He was interviewed on nationwide radio and television shows, including *The Daily Show* and National Public Radio, and ran for President in 2004 and 2008. Gene was also a talented artist who produced many charming landscapes, and he created life-sized painted wood carvings of cartoonish characters that decorate Vashon still. A couple of them can be seen along the main highway beginning a little north of town and extending south to near Courthouse Square. He was a proponent of alternative transportation and could often be seen riding up and down the highway on his personal Segway.

I met Gene in about 2005 after I had completed a linocut print that poked fun at one of his creations, a tiny Norwegian church north of town that he advertised as a site for weddings. The church building is so small that I imagined normal people would have to kneel to get in, and so I made a print that claimed that gnome weddings were held there every Saturday at midnight. The two gnomes I put in the image both had beards (there are no female gnomes, are there?), but on one I put a wedding dress. I thought it was a good example of "Vashon funk," but realized that Gene might take offense, so I called him to ask his permission to show the print.

Gene invited me over to his house and I opened the folder containing the print. He chuckled and asked about the printing technique (block printing), and then said he didn't mind if I exhibited the print except that he was a little concerned that the gnomes were both men. He didn't want to give the wrong impression about Vashon. We chatted about that for a while and explored the existential nature of mythical creatures, and then he graciously approved my work and complimented me besides. From then on, we'd exchange greetings and short conversations whenever we'd see each other.

I can imagine that some might think Gene would not appreciate being included in a chapter on Watering Holes. It's too late to ask him for permission, but I would point out that Gene fought watering holes and alcohol producers during much of his life and was commonly in their presence. You can't fight alcohol unless you face it nose-to-nose, and it was a good portion of his life's work. Given that, I think it's more than appropriate to not only include this story of him here, but to close with a statement from Gene: "Your kids need you sober."

You can't disagree with that.

Vashion Fashion (the Gospel according to Cindy Hoyt)

NEWCOMERS WHO'VE BEEN here for about fifteen seconds have noticed that what happens on the Fashion Week runways of Paris, New York, or even Seattle has NOTHING to do with what the locals wear on Vashon Island. This doesn't mean we're a lot of hayseeds; it simply means that our down-to-earth lifestyles call for something a little more...earthy. "Form follows function" on Vashon as NOWHERE else (except maybe at South Pole science stations).

Let's start with footwear. Most island roads and driveways are long gravelly pothole-riddled booby-traps. In winter, the potholes are filled with opaque water laced with raccoon-borne diseases. And at night there are no streetlights to reflect in those puddles and show you where to step. This makes it easy to spot a female island visitor without even looking above her ankles. Her three-inch heels are broken, her leather uppers are rock-scarred, and mud oozes out of the open toes that looked so fantastic on her at the mall. And if she's here to visit friends, she'll wonder why she even bothered; everyone here is aware of the local conditions, so they remove their shoes as soon as they get inside the door. Your best bet for footwear around here is knee-high muck boots over the most adorable pair of socks you can find, because it's the SOCKS that everyone will see.

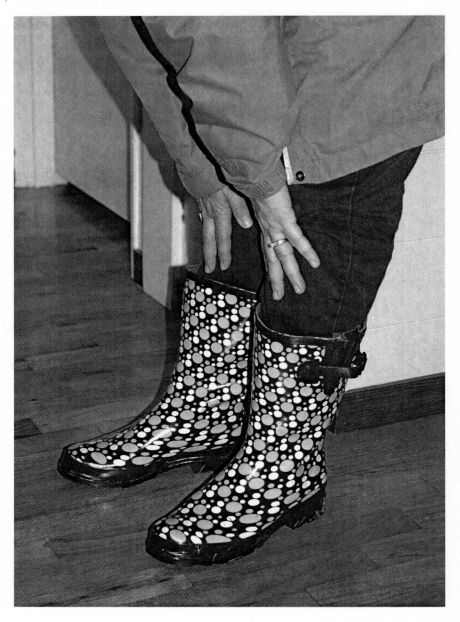

The most essential article in your personal wardrobe if you are a resident of the Pacific Northwest.

Above the feet, as well, the earthy theme prevails: our local color palette ranges the full spectrum between pale moss and dark brown. Inside those parameters, hey! Anything goes! Get crazy! (Fashionista's note: it's dandy to break out your black duds for special occasions. OK, OK, it's mandatory. You shouldn't have to find that out the hard way.)

There are two vivid exceptions to the color code: 1) high school sporting events and 2) hunting season.

The Vashon Pirates' team colors are forest green (logical) and Yellow Cab (Where'd THAT come from?? We don't even HAVE taxis!). Anyone attending a game will want to wear a T-shirt or sweatshirt in that bright, bright yellow. They will be boosting the team's morale AND visible at night on the aforementioned unlit roads. Failing to do either can be life-threatening.

Speaking of life-threatening: hunting season on Vashon extends from September through December. Separate weeks are reserved for bow-hunters, muzzle-loaders (we kid you not) and semi-automatics (we kid you). Although the trailheads in the popular Island Center Forest have loaner vests in eye-catching international orange, there have been a few incidents where cars parked in residents' driveways and even the homes attached to the driveways have sustained collateral damage. Therefore we recommend that whether you're going for a walk in the woods, picking up a latte at a downtown bistro, or even just taking the air on the porch of your B&B, it's a good idea to add a touch of orange to your wardrobe, even if it's NOT one of your colors. And that goes double for your dog!

Next up: casual wear. Wait, now that we think about it, that's pretty much the entire chapter. Island ladies tend toward slightly-pilled zip-front cardigans over stretch-denim jeans with dirt ground into the right knee and grace notes of mud splatters on the cuffs. This versatile outfit goes smoothly from weeding the vegetables to milking the goats, which is why it's such a favorite with our many farm stand operators. Of course, every now and then you'll see a gal who's really put together; you know, wearing pants that actually match one of the colors in her Machu Picchu sweatshirt, and hiking boots she didn't forget to waterproof. This is as rare around here as real jewelry, so have your camera handy!

Other island women who enjoy making an effort can be fashion "sensible" on a budget. With a blazer from Wendy's Weathered Wear over a Granny's Attic turtleneck, rounded out with slacks from Luna Bella, you'll be the belle of the Blue Heron for around $13.50. You'll be looking good and still have enough left over to buy a ferry ticket to the mainland to pick up lingerie, which is never as much fun when acquired second-hand.

As to accessories: you'll quickly discover that the island version of a $200 Dolce & Gabbana handbag is the $1.95 Thriftway shopping bag. The good news is at that price, you can afford the entire collection: green, black, natural and Susan G. Komen pink for year-round style. And don't miss IGA's green bag with its red and white center splash. Just the thing for the holidays!

Just so you fellows don't think we're leaving you out, here's YOUR fashion prescription for ANY island function at ANY time of year: a button-down shirt of indeterminate color and pattern tucked into a pair of khaki Dockers, finished off with a pair of white beach-stained sneakers. But don't forget the *Rule of Black* at formal events; this is the time to break out those dress black sneakers that are buried under the pile of unused neckties on the top shelf of your closet.

That's about all you need to know about how to "blend in" with the locals here on Vashon Island. But we do want to leave you with one final note: Never wear white after Labor Day, and on Vashon, never wear white after BREAKFAST!

Things to Do (yawn)

THERE ARE LOTS of things to do on Vashon, especially if you confine your list to things your grandparents would enjoy. There is the Farmer's Market in the middle of town on Saturdays (in the summer), visiting the History Museum, and a number of parks have charming trails where you can walk through the woods or to the beach. You can also bicycle in relative safety, rent a kayak at Jensen Point, and attend any number of musical performances on weekend nights. Bird watching is fun. You can even take up thumbing a ride for sport. Seriously.

If you want to find out more about these recreational opportunities (except the thumbing), I suggest visiting the websites for the Vashon-Maury Island Chamber of Commerce and the Vashon-Maury Island Community Council. Both have links that will allow you to research fun things to do, whether it's in a park or a place of business. Vashon Allied Arts, our local non-profit art organization, hosts lots of fun outings and performances, and they have a web site, too.

Another great resource is a pamphlet entitled *Destination Vashon* that is published every year by *The Beachcomber*. You can find a stack of them (they are free) at most places where you can find the free newspapers and other pamphlets, such as on all of the ferry boats and at the entrances to larger businesses like grocery stores.

Destination Vashon is the closest thing we have to an island travel guide, however it does read a bit like it was written by the Chamber of Commerce. If you want more suggestions of things to do, you'll find them there. If you want the inside skinny, you probably won't, because the inside skinny is not always good for business.

Or you can always just invest 75 cents and buy *The Beachcomber* (our weekly paper that comes out every Wednesday) because in each issue they list events and performances for the coming week. Many events are also published in our emergency backup paper, *The Loop*, which is published twice a month. It is also available free at the appropriate places.

Another reference that you can be sure no one else will recommend is a book that just came out called *Codex Benthos*, written by a sort-of-local character named Cecil Benthos. This book is a catalog of lost mines, buried treasures, unsolved mysteries, and unexplained oddities for Vashon and Maury Islands. I suspect that some of the stories are "embellished," but I do know for a fact that some of them are "true." There is even an account of one treasure that actually was found by two ambitious youngsters (who are real), so there is always the chance that you could take a weekend and find fame and fortune following the clues in this book. There is also a chance that you could be struck by a meteorite. You can ask at bookstores for a copy or order one online.

Something that used to be a lot of fun to do on Vashon was to sneak up onto the Thriftway sign and rearrange the moveable letters. Not that I ever did this, but some other creative folks did it from time to time, treating us to bawdy comments or rude remarks on that sign and others as well. One morning I drove down the highway and discovered four moveable-letter signs that had been so altered. I cannot quote what they said, but you can guess that it was something sophomoric.

Sadly, this past year both Thriftway and Island Lumber traded in their old iconic signs (that could be vandalized) for high-tech computerized signs of the kind that give you a headache if you look for too long. Lots of people were up in arms about the new signs because of their glaring non-island nature, but it seems to me that the new signs are just another example of evolution in action.

Look at it this way: there are two grocery stores on the island. There are also two hardware stores. The available market (humans receptive to advertising) is limited in size. Each of these stores is competing for dominance in the economy, sort of like each male is competing for dominance with available females. We males (and I count myself in that group) grow more colorful feathers or bellow louder, and the girls come flocking 'round our doorsteps. These two stores do the same thing by flaunting more colorful signs or more annoying advertising, anything to get our attention. And certainly those two signs have gotten a LOT of attention, meaning they are evolutionarily successful! By all rights, we should be crowding into Thriftway and Island Lumber and throwing our money at the cashiers! It may be that I already do that, but I assure you it's not because of the signs.

So if you don't like these Christmassy signs, fight the animal inside you and do something that would make the signs ineffective. For instance, every time a new advertisement goes up, walk into the competing store and buy something. Vashon is full of contrarians, so be contrary!

Or I...I mean WE...could figure out a way to make the signs read something else. I'm told it can be a challenge to climb up and rearrange "Asparagus, two stalks for a dollar" into something clever with no leftover letters. Thanks to modern technology, we can avoid the rickety ladder and dive straight into the word exercise. It could even be part of the high school English curriculum! No vandal left behind.

Of course, with the new computerized signs it helps if you know the system password. Because I can't remember mine, I keep it on a sticky note affixed to my computer. I assume the aging folks at these businesses do the same, so it's just a matter of time before we can sneak a peek and bust the sign game wide open.

This woman is NOT reprogramming the Thriftway sign! At least not this time.

Until then, you might find yourself sitting around most of the time thinking about doing something recreational, but never really doing it. Instead, you might rationalize your time on the island as an opportunity to organize your thoughts, charge up your batteries, and begin a career as a writer. With luck, you won't discover that you're becoming a crank.

When I was a lot younger, I enjoyed reading short stories and essays by old guys who probably were thought by their contemporaries to be cranks. Mark Twain, Bret Harte, James Thurber, and others made my middle school years bearable. I could laugh at the foibles of humanity and feel mature and superior while being teased by a 13-year-old girl in homeroom. When I got a "D" on one of Miss Ruel's history tests, I could retreat into my Walter Mitty world and imagine that I was working for Special Branch after 007 went missing.

But these old guys didn't get to their pinnacles of American Literature easily. I know now that it took years of practice and lots of rejection before they could overcome the ridicule of their friends and acquaintances. It also took a lot of practice and years of rejection before they figured out that no one wants to read the rantings of a guy who is upset. Constructive criticism is one thing; rantings are something else entirely. These guys had to figure out ways to write about sensitive topics that just barely brushed their surfaces. Had they gone out bicycling or kayaking instead, they'd have lost their edge.

With age comes experience and wisdom. With age also comes self confidence enough to look people in the eye and not give a rat's arse what they think of you, all the while with a piece of spinach stuck in your front teeth. Sadly, it is this newfound self-confidence that causes some of us to take up writing (or any expressive art form) at an age when we have something to say but little experience in how best to say it. I imagine that Galileo was an old crank, as was Plato, Socrates, and Martin Luther. And look where it got these people; they're all dead!

For a lot of us who are "of an age," the things we often write about are "laments about the inevitable passage of time and the loss of youthful innocence." By this I mean we are pissed off at the kids.

When I was a kid, my favorite spot, other than out in the woods looking for fossils, was curled up in front of our 20-inch black-and-white television with a glass bottle of Coca-Cola where I could watch old horror films on Saturday afternoons. My father would point out the window at the grass in the backyard, and then say it was my day to fire up the old push-it-yourself Toro. I'd stall at least until Dracula was toasted by the rising Sun.

The kids today have way more distractions of that sort. I can't even begin to list all the technological devices in our house, mainly because I don't know what they are, but I do know that the kids in my world spend most of their waking hours (and some of their sleeping hours) peering into a screen.

I can blame anyone who is not in my generation, and some who are, for this development. But really, we are all responsible. The kids today were prepared for years of screen-peering by their parents, who grew up peering into a television. The parents were prepared for TV-peering by their parents who grew up staring at a radio. The grandparents stared at a Victrola. The great-grandparents stared at something else, possibly each other.

The trend is obvious. At time progresses, we are becoming more detached from each other with respect to physical presence, and simultaneously more attached via technology. It has gotten so bad at our house that we call the kids to dinner by sending them an instant message, and this is when the kids are literally in the next room. They grab their plates and run back to their screens, so that all of their friends can instantly know that Mom made a disgusting vegetarian dish. They do it by using TXT that looks something like this: "DUDE DINNR SUX I H8 TOFU BRGRS." This kind of writing would have killed my eighth-grade English teacher and simultaneously caused her to roll over in her grave.

I could rant more, but instead I'd like to offer a few hints for simple pleasures that you can enjoy in our modern world that don't require ANY technological devices. Get back to the Earth and reconnect, is what I say! Try these things, even if you came to Vashon to write:

1. *Walk the dog* (Remember the biodegradable poop bag and the reflective vest. If after dark, put a flashing LED light on the dog's collar.)
2. *Go dancing* (Wear a face mask during flu season and wash your hands after. If you are over 45, you might want a portable heart monitor that is connected via a satellite link to your doctor's paging service.)
3. *Let your wife or husband take you out to dinner* (Check the Health Department first for reports about the restaurant. Their internet site has a complaint form if your experience is less than wonderful.)
4. *Plant a vegetable garden* (Pictures of your growing plants are fun to post on the web.)

5. *Chase the deer away from your garden* (There is a deer-hate list server you can find with a Google search.)
6. *Start a collection* (You can have the world's biggest collection of whatever in just days if you search on eBay. Who needs garage sales?)
7. *Discover a good beer* (There are thousands worldwide, and you can order them online and pay through PayPal.)
8. *Have a quiet discussion around the fireplace* (Use the opportunity to burn credit card receipts and other records to prevent identity theft.)
9. *Take a trip to an exotic place far away from Vashon* (Remember to take only three ounces of shampoo, and leave the pocket knives at home. Check for terrorist travel advisories at the State Department's home page. Make sure your cell phone will work there, and investigate web access to update your peeps via Facebook and MySpace. Update your internet security software. You may need a water purifier, a GPS unit, and a medical reference device.)
10. *If you are single, get out there and meet someone new* (My wife and I met through Science Connection. I tried five other internet dating services at the time and my experiences would fill another book, mostly with horror stories.)

It may seem like it, but I'm not entirely against computers. I like mine for writing because it's way easier to correct my mistakes than what I used before, an IBM Selectric. The old Royal typewriter my father had was even harder to use, but back then I had fingers of steel. It took a lot of pressure to type one letter on the Royal. Using the same amount of energy today, I can produce an entire essay in Microsoft Word. If this trend continues, humans will evolve really small hands. With voice recognition, we could get rid of hands entirely.

I plan to avoid voice-recognition devices for just that reason. I kind of like my hands, and that I can hold my wife with them and pat the dog. She and Bubby are out walking as I write this, so I think I'll text her to see where they are. If she texts me her GPS coordinates, I can take them an extra biodegradable bag. But first I have to chase some deer away from the tomatoes.

Real Things to See (Momma, don't take my Kodachrome)

ONE OF THE great things about being a scientist is that I know lots of things that other people don't. I don't enjoy rubbing it in, but when I see a controversy erupt in the community, there are times when I can offer a concise explanation that just stops traffic cold. And there are times when I'm also correct. But it's easy to be correct in this chapter, because there are a lot of things to see on Vashon. Most of them are pretty dull, but there are enough interesting ones to give you a good excuse for a day trip or two.

What I'd like to do here is list some of the things everyone comes to see (this is a travel guide, after all) as well as some things that no one comes to see. The latter category will prove to be the most interesting.

If you've ever seen pictures of Vashon, you more than likely have seen a picture of the lighthouse at **Pt. Robinson**. The lighthouse is in a park that is administered by the Vashon Park District, and it draws a lot of visitors despite that fact that it looks like lots of the other light-houses scattered around Puget Sound. I am thinking this is probably because they were all built about the same time by about the same folks, but I may be mistaken. In any case, a signal light was first es-tablished at Pt. Robinson in 1855, and the current tower was built in 1915. The nearby houses (which were Coast Guard residences and are now vacation rentals) were added in 1907 and 1918. It's a good place to take the kids on a sunny day, but don't let your dog off of his leash. The lighthouse was also written up in Berkeley Breathed's book

Red Ranger Comes Calling as the home of Santa. I personally do not think Santa lives there; I think he just vacations on Vashon during the summer.

Pt. Robinson lighthouse. There are literally millions of pictures like this one.

There are several other shoreline parks maintained by the park district and the county. The largest is King County's **Maury Island Marine Park**, which except for some great trails is largely undeveloped. There's a parking lot off of SW 244th where you can safely leave your car while you hike down the hill to the shoreline. It's a good walk if you're in reasonable shape, but beware of the climb back up. Dogs are also welcome, but they are supposed to be leashed. NEVER let your dog loose on the beach during those months when you might encounter seal pups, which is during the spring and summer.

Recently, King County purchased the Glacier NW quarry property that is similar in size and nearly adjacent to the Maury Island Marine Park. The county intends to create a regional park and restore much of the quarry, but that work is years off. In the meantime, walk-in access is allowed.

If you join the Vashon-Maury Island Caving Club, you can learn about all the caves on the island, the locations of which are secret except to club members. And you can get this great patch!

A shoreline park that is privately held (but is nevertheless open to the public) is **KVI Beach** at Ellisport. This beach is owned by Fisher Broadcasting (hence the large transmission tower) but folks are welcome to use it provided you take home your trash and clean up after your dog. Dogs often run free here, and lots of folks take their canine pals to KVI just for that reason. So if you are not crazy about being sniffed all over by a soaking wet black lab, you might want to stay home. Parking is abysmal, and take care to not block a driveway or be offensive to the folks who live adjacent. This is probably the most kid-friendly beach on Vashon (not accounting for wet noses or dog-stolen hamburgers), with lots of sand and a great shallow tidal channel in which the little ones can play (with supervision, of course). For the birders, eagles frequently hang out on the transmission tower. It's also a favorite place for scuba diving, and I have seen folks looking for coins with a metal detector at KVI. I searched for treasure there once myself, and I could tell you that I found three gold coins and a diamond ring, but I won't. If you see any broken glass, clean it up, please; our parents and dog lovers will thank you. And there are no toilets there, but you can practice your "holding."

The famous **bike-in-the-tree** is something all serious travelers to Vashon should see, and coincidently it was also featured in *Red Ranger Comes Calling*. It is a regular looking kid's bicycle that was wedged up in the crotch of a fir tree years ago and subsequently abandoned. Over the years, the tree grew around it and completely encased the frame of the bike, so that it looks like the bicycle was somehow magically inserted through the tree. With exposure to the weather and vandals, the bike has suffered over the years, but loyal fans have occasionally replaced stolen parts. Still, there's only so much you can do with rusty steel, so the bicycle is now somewhat fragile. For that reason, I'm not going to tell you where it is. You'll have to ask someone else. When you do find it, take care not to damage it. Take only photos and leave only footprints.

The famous bike in the tree is about 10 feet off the ground.

For years, most islanders had no clue as to how the bicycle got into the tree. We could tell that it had been there for some time, probably close to two generations. But why anyone would leave a perfectly good bicycle stuck up in a tree for that long was hard for us to understand, given as we are to both dispelling mysteries and reducing waste.

It was in late 2009 that an article in *The Beachcomber* finally set the record straight. According to that article, a longtime island family claimed to be responsible, stating that the bicycle belonged to Don Puz, who left the bike in the tree in 1954, forgot about it, and never went looking for it. How the bicycle got to be about 10 feet in the air was not explained. Don had to be eight or nine years old at the time, because he graduated from Vashon High School in 1963. His mother, Helen (aged 97), explained that Don and his friends were playing in the woods together and Don was the only child who had ridden his bicycle there. When the other boys left, Don left his bike behind, walking home with his pals. "Apparently, he wasn't too excited about that bike," she is reported to have said.

After the bike was discovered and made headlines, Helen and Don paid it a visit. Don recalled, "I recognized it immediately, because I don't think I've ever seen another one like it." Don received the bicycle as a donation after the family home burnt down, he said, but it wasn't his favorite because it had solid rubber tires and he was too big to ride it. "Probably as much as I detested the little thing, I just gave it a toss and forgot about it, and then denied knowing where it was," he was reported to have said. One wonders if after all those years, his mother tanned his hide for having "lost" such a good bike.

Not far from the bicycle tree (oops...I almost gave it away) are some of **Gene Amondson's carved sculptures.** Gene is described elsewhere in this book. At the risk of being redundant let me say that he was a local artist who painted as well as sculpted. His sculptures are mostly cartoonish characters that were carved from cedar logs and then painted. At least three can be sighted along Vashon Highway beginning north of town next to the little church (which is also his creation) and continuing south of town. There is also one in the lobby of the U.S. Bank. With the exception of the one in the bank, these sculptures are weathering fast, so make sure and see them before they are gone.

One of Gene Amondson's sculptures.

Another sculpture that you will drive past on the highway just south of town is a large metal sculpture at Court House Square that was created by islander Julie Speidel, who is a nationally renowned metal sculptor. The work is entitled "The Gathering" and was commissioned for both the Court House Square and Vashon College. It was intended to portray the idea of community and people working together for a common goal. It's a striking piece by a famous artist, so I recommend you stop and take a look.

Yet another sculpture (or artifact?), a **crashed (or landed) UFO**, is located at the Vashon Municipal Airport off of Cove Road just west of 107th. The entrance gate to the airport is often closed and locked, so you may have to park alongside Cove Road (be careful doing this) and walk in. Take care to walk only on the roadways and not on the runway. The UFO is located just north of the last hanger on the east side of the runway. It's my 3rd favorite thing on the island, trailing my wife and my dog.

According to an article in the *Seattle Post-Intelligencer* by Jon Hahn (from 2002), the spacecraft was "found" alongside the runway by locals who were clearing brush. Mike Sweeney, a local private pilot, stated that *"This is pretty much how we found it, pitched over into the dirt, when we were clearing brush alongside the runway."* Mike noted that the craft's escape hatch measures just 8 inches across, suggesting that the crew was somewhat smaller than the average island resident.

Mike also reported to Jon Hahn that some islanders suspect the aliens have inbred with the general population, which could explain the widely held perception that Vashon Island residents are from another planet. I'm thinking that even Vashonistas would prefer not to mate with something only eight inches high, but I could be wrong there.

A crashed UFO at the Vashon Municipal Airport.

Far be it from me to discount another islander's wacky and totally crazy theory, no matter how amazingly stupid it is, but I'm a just a little skeptical about the idea that this spacecraft crashed at the airport. I mean, really, there is a perfectly good set of runway lights at the airport, so how could a civilization calling itself "advanced" screw up so royally and crash to the *side* of the runway?? That's just nuts. More likely, the spacecraft was intentionally positioned that way to lead us into thinking the aliens are klutzs so we would not fear them. For all we know, they could already be in charge of the Community Council.

But if there are any little green men (or ladies) running around the island, they had better stay away from **Wolftown**. Wolftown is a not-for-profit organization that rehabilitates injured or orphaned wild animals and returns them to the wild. They rescue all species, including eagles, but they specialize in predators, especially wild canids. As far as I know, they have not returned any canids to the wild on the island, but one can always hope. In the meantime, I know they assist with "cleaning up" some of the many road-killed deer that litter the island. You can visit Wolftown (and safely see the wolves) but you must arrange a tour in advance. See what they do, and contact them, at www.wolftown.org.

Another locally famous artwork, and one that you will see as soon as you enter town, is the **Vashon history mural** that decorates the entire back wall of the U.S. Bank building on the northwest corner of Bank Road and Vashon Highway (the very center of town). The mural was painted by island artist William Forrester, assisted by local grade-schoolers who painted some of the birds in the margins.

The mural was commissioned by U.S. Bank, and it supposedly commemorates 100 years of banking on the island (minus the recent mortgage debacle), but more than that it captures a century of island life and a good number of famous islanders and historic events. For those of you who are not intimately familiar with Vashon history, there is a legend to the mural posted on the east side of the bank building, adjacent to the sidewalk.

William Forrester's mural on the back of the U.S. Bank building.

Artist William Forrester is an accomplished painter as well as a farmer, and he told the crowd at the unveiling in early 2009 that the mural was for him the work of a lifetime. In addition, he said that he was thankful to have the opportunity to use his talents to benefit the community, and that "No children were hurt in the making of this mural." That is certainly more than I can say for some of my artistic ventures.

The old **Vashon roasterie** is the last place I'll send you in this chapter, figuring that after a day of traipsing around the island looking as sculptures and wolves and the like, you'll need a good cup of coffee. There is good coffee available elsewhere, but not in such an interesting (and creaky) old building.

The Vashon roasterie is at the corner of Vashon Highway SW and SW Cemetery Road, a mile or two south of the town center. Jim Stewart of Stewart Brothers Coffee (which later became Seattle's Best Coffee) did a lot of his early company development here, and it was also the site of his original coffee shop, The Wet Whisker. The roasterie currently houses another coffee company, The Vashon Island Coffee Roasterie, which shares the building with Minglement, an organic health food and herb store.

Minglement has such a large collection of exotic herbs and spices that it is somewhat like being inside a Chinese apothecary. In fact, it reminds me of the herbs and medicines peddled by the "witches" in La Paz, Bolivia. On certain streets in La Paz, these ladies will sell you medicines and potions for most complaints, and magical concoctions as well. You can buy local herbs, spices, coca leaves, brightly colored minerals, carved totems, and even a dried llama fetus to bury under your new home (for good luck). When I first saw a dried llama fetus, I was struck by its resemblance to Hollywood's depiction of alien beings. I guess for that reason is it too bad we can't buy one here, because they would fit in really well with the UFO at the airport. I remember that they were only about eight inches tall.

This lady does not yet work at Minglement, but it would be cool if she did.

Recurring Events (do we have to go to the Strawberry Festival again??)

AS YOU MIGHT expect in any small community, there are a number of events throughout the year that are hosted annually, and that draw tourists to enhance the local economy. Of course, money is not the primary motivation for these events, despite the fact that most of them are either organized by the Chamber of Commerce or involve buying things after you are served alcohol. Rather, they are individual and unique expressions of the artistic and social values and of our progressive community. And I have this bridge for sale...

One of my favorites is the First Friday Gallery Cruise. The first Friday of every month, art galleries and small shops that exhibit island artists are open late (6 till 9 PM) to allow folks to walk around and view the offerings. Complimentary wine is sometimes available (one small glass per person per venue, provided a state-licensed server is on hand) and local musicians often grace the crowds with song. I know it sounds like First Friday could easily turn into a rowdy street party, but really it's just a quiet gathering of art lovers and other folks out looking for a free drink. I've never seen a person "streak" on First Friday, for example, but I suppose one can always hope. I'd do it myself if I didn't "stand out" in a crowd.

Most other recurring events occur only once or twice a year. There are lots of charity auctions, for example, that are held every year after much fanfare and advertising build-up. Vashon Island Pet Protectors (VIPP for short) has a great one, as does Vashon Allied Arts. The schools also benefit from a PTSA auction, and there is another for the Community Care Center (the old folks' home, or as my mother, who lives in one, calls it, Geezerama). There are, in fact, so many charity auctions that it is difficult or even impossible to attend more than one or two, especially if you buy something.

For years, the VIPP auction has been my favorite, usually because the artwork that I donate sells well to that crowd. But all of them are lots of fun and all operate pretty much the same way. Island residents are asked to donate goods or services to auction off, and then they are asked to come to the auction (paying an admission charge to get in), and buy lots of stuff, including their own donated items if absolutely necessary. Food and alcohol are involved, and the drinks are cheap. It's a lot of fun provided you don't get caught up in the bidding wars after having too many beers and finish the evening with both a headache and an empty wallet, which happens to me every single time. I once bought a sailboat cruise for something like $400 while my wife Margaret was in the restroom, thinking it was romantic and that she'd be pleased when she discovered my surprise. To say that she was surprised would be inaccurate.

Two other annual events that I can recommend are the annual spelling bee hosted by the Vashon Community Scholarship Foundation held around the end of January, and the Oscars Night Party, held (surprisingly) on Oscars night. Both events are usually held at the Vashon Theatre.

For the spelling bee, teams of spellers dress up in outrageous costumes and attempt to look smart by spelling the most words. For Oscars Night, singles, couples, and occasionally teams attempt to look smart by dressing in costumes, fancy clothes, or pajamas. Both events are a hoot.

At the Oscars Night Party, Margaret and I once took the prize for the best-dressed adult couple, and we've gone several times since. But this year was the first time we competed in the spelling bee. Our team name was "Miner Typo" and we dressed up as hard-rock miners with hard hats and picks. It was funny that we were listed in the program as "Minor Typo," which was a typo itself. In typical fashion, Margaret studied and I didn't, but we lost anyway.

Stepping out at the Oscars Night celebration.

Or you can go in your pajamas.

July 4th is also a big day for Vashon, with a first-class fireworks display in Quartermaster Harbor, paid for by someone other than me but who I can't name now because the donors (and we thank them whoever they are) are usually anonymous. But the fireworks are not all that is loud on the 4th. Early in the morning of every July 4th, around about daybreak, there is a hydrofoil race. These are small, extremely noisy boats that sound like very angry bees with a megaphone. The boats race all the way around the islands, insuring that you'll hear the race no matter where you live. It is literally the most grating noise you'll experience during the entire year, and it arrives just before your alarm clock goes off, prompting some folks (like ME) to be a little irritated. "Obnoxious Boat Racing, Every July 4th," is what the travel poster should read.

Throughout the year, there are also lots of organized tours of various things on the islands. There are tours of the lavender farms, tours of spectacular gardens, tours of art studios, chicken coops, septic systems, haunted houses, crime scenes, places where UFOs landed, and places that claim to be the true center of the known universe. I can't vouch for the veracity of the last four, but I have attended some of the other tours, including the art studio tour (which is held twice a year), and I have never been disappointed. I have found that for the most part, Vashon artists are amazingly creative, extremely talented, and usually not harmful to society.

The Christmas season is also replete with staged...I mean ORGANIZED...events that thrill adults and children alike, including the widely heralded Christmas Parade and Tree Lighting Ceremony, held the first weekend in December. There is a good chance that the tree will actually light up when the switch is thrown, but to be honest, in the years that I have attended the ceremony, the tree lighting has never proceeded according to plan. We have actually taken bets on what part of the tree would not light when it was plugged in, providing yet another source of holiday fun. If you divide the tree into fourths, you have a 25% chance of winning. Don't bet more than a six-pack of beer, is my advice.

The mother of all recurring events is the Strawberry Festival. If you are on Vashon during July, there is no friggin' way you can avoid going. If your wife/husband doesn't drag you there, your kids will, or your neighbor will shame you into going. You dog will even sulk if you don't go; that's how ingrained it is in Vashonites.

Typical reaction upon learning it is time for yet another Strawberry Festival.

For those of you who are uninitiated, Strawberry Festival is an annual street fair with many booths selling on-island and off-island goods, accompanied by two parades (the largest one being on Saturday) and lots of music venues scattered throughout town. As usual, I never want to go, but this past summer our dog trainer encouraged me to attend with our dog, Bubby, because he needed the exposure. Also, my wife reminded me that attending the SF is one of those implied duties of a faithful spouse. How can you argue with that?

On Saturday of that fateful weekend, Margaret left the house early without breakfast to take her daughter to town for the parade, while I made some delicious coffee and enjoyed a leisurely meal. Bubby and I took our time because any marriage counselor will tell you it's important to make time for yourselves on the weekend. After our leisurely breakfast, Bubby and I arrived in town and parked the car on the highway just 15 minutes before the parade was scheduled to start. Fortunately, the schedule was largely imaginary because Bubby and I had to walk in about two miles from our parking place.

I remember the hike really well, and the first float, which I think was a train or a fire engine, but after that my memory was compromised by a blow on the head from a thrown lollypop, so the rest of this report may appear a bit scattered.

It may also appear scattered because I was stressed keeping Bubby under control. He did really well around the people (and the food they dropped) but he was a little short with some of the big dogs who wanted to check him out. At one point, one of the guide-dogs-in-training came up from behind and tried to sniff his posterior. As pleasurable as that may sound, Bubby did not take it kindly. I responded with a quick controlling maneuver, but not before one of our island's many attorneys clicked a photo of me with her cell phone. I am guessing that festivals offer many opportunities for potential litigation.

What I remember about the floats is that they were a little different from previous years. For instance the "Old Guys On Tractors" Club seemed to include a lot of younger-looking people. Also, the Pirates Football float (Vashon High School) was pulled by local contractor Lewis Roggenbuck rather than the Glacier NW quarrying company (who pulled them the previous year), which meant we could applaud for both the team and the guys pulling the float.

But there were a couple of things that threw me off. One was the Pirate Band's selection of "On, Wisconsin" as Vashon's official fight song. Okay, so it's another "W" state...but.... And then there was the second fire engine that we discovered later was actually in the middle of the parade. We assumed it signaled the end until my wife Margaret noticed another marching group about three blocks back. It was a bunch of politicians who had fielded about as many candidates for the parade as the town did parade-watchers. I actually saw one of the politicians marching in the wrong direction. I won't tell you who that was, but his/her name is followed with an (R).

The Thriftway Precision Shopping Carts Team was impeccable that year, and fortunately we were near the end of the parade route so their carts had already been emptied of the canned goods that they threw to the crowd. I could not have stood another whack on the head.

Shortly after, there was a large gap..."dead time" as they call it in the radio business...that we thought for sure meant the parade was finally over. Bubby and I wandered off to use the little boy's room/bush and just as we were done, we heard the sultry rhythms of the samba dancers. If you haven't seen them, you should, because they are a team of charming and scantily clad ladies doing provocative dances, who appeared to have been accompanied this time by at least one topless guy. At least I'm hoping that was a guy.

The parade "finally" ended with some aging rock stars on the back of a truck and we wandered off to check out the 148 off-island vendors and the 16 on-island vendors. There were also a lot of on-island bands playing, although we noticed that most of them seemed to be composed of the same musicians. Our favorite, The Church House Band from the Church of Great Rain, announced that they had to cancel because their drummer had a gig with another band in the same time slot.

Just in case this happens again, I'd like to offer my services as a stand-in musician. I don't play anything, but I figure the others can cover for me. How hard can it be?

Romantic Places (falling or failing in love or sex on Vashon)

I KNOW I am not the first to point out that Vashon Island is a great place to fall in love. Based on what I've seen during my many travels through the Pacific Northwest, I'd have to extend that accolade to the entire region, except for Enumclaw unless you're a "lover of horses."

It was not until I met The Marvelous Miss M that I realized I wanted to live only on Vashon because she told me this was where we were going to live. I was holding out for Wallingford, but the streets there were too narrow for her van, which has since met its demise by hitting a deer head-on. In Wallingford, I could have dined in Thai restaurants, gone to the Art Museum on a whim, and walked up the street to get my mocha, but c'est la vie.

Regardless of where you are on the west side of the Cascades, it's a romantic's paradise. The filtered sunlight (nearly 10 days a year) and gentle breezes more than compensate for the wind and rain the rest of the time. When Spring finally arrives in July, the weather is so beautiful that you want to rip off your layered fleeces and get a terrible sunburn! Even Republicans feel the magic and are inspired to cuddle up and kiss, which based upon our last 50 years of Presidents is not something they normally do. The Democrats seem to make up for that deficit.

When you take politicians out of the database, it's clear that there are two age groups where singleness peaks: people in their 20s who have not yet found Mr./Miss Right, and people in their 40s who have given the sack to Mr./Mrs. Right. Vashon demographics are weighted toward the older bunch, so I address my comments to those folks. (Note to the ladies: I know there aren't many men on Vashon who are both single and desirable, but stay positive and you might find one with both a job and a pulse. With luck, he won't be from Tacoma.)

Let's assume that you've found a likely victim...I mean partner... and that you're ready to show him/her the uniqueness of living on Vashon and helping make your house payment. The next step is to orchestrate a romantic weekend on the island with visits to one or two romantic places. THIS is where I can help, because listed below, for the first time ever, is a selection of the most romantic places and most romantic things to do EVER in the history of Vashon Island, or even longer! I've numbered them so that in years to come, you can catch your sweetie's attention, wink, and say "How about a number four?"

1. KVI Beach is always popular for a romantic walk. Watch out for the dog poop and the teenagers who like to carouse and drink at the far end. On the plus side, if you take the dog you might stumble on a dead seal on which he can roll.

2. The Recycling Center at the dump is a great place to meet an environmentally friendly person and also check out how many wine bottles they go through. Don't bother dressing up, but do affect a wind-blown, outdoorsy look. If you stop for coffee after, you'll be able to get that smell out of your nose.

3. Church. My father always said if I wanted to meet a good woman, I'd go to church. The problem was I didn't want to meet a "good" woman, I wanted to meet a "great" woman, and I just couldn't think about deep, dark sinnin' while sitting on a pew. But I suppose if you were in the back row....

4. Speaking of the back row, there is always the monthly Community Council meeting for people into Public Displays of Affection. Most of the folks in front of you will be really into the discussion, so you can get away with murder. If *Voice of Vashon* is taping it, you might be on TV!

5. The Post Office. Imagine standing in line and saying things

to your cutie like "I'd go postal for your kisses," or "I've got your 'Special Delivery' right here." At the very least, you can make the people around you uncomfortable or even down-right nauseous. Loads of fun.

6. The coffee grinders at Thriftway. If you're going to grind coffee, why not do it while grinding?

7. Any of the island B&Bs are great for a night away from the kids. You can have fun making up comments for the guest book like "Our passion was driven to new heights by your choice of pillows," or "We didn't know a bathroom fixture could be used as a sex toy!" Pick one on the other side of the island from where you live, and register under a false name. It's more exciting that way, and liability is minimized.

8. King County's Maury Island Marine Park is a great place for a good walk and to show off your invertebrate identification skills. Limpets, chitons, and isopods cavort there aplenty, and you can point them all out just like a real Park Ranger. It's also remote enough for nude activities, but big enough to get lost in. Take some extra sunscreen in case you get separated from your sweetie. I learned this the hard way.

9. First Friday Art Walk is a good place to get free wine (in amazingly small portions) and impress your date by acting like a snooty art critic. You can look down your nose at artworks you could have sworn were done by kindergarteners...but for some reason are priced at over $1000. Be careful what you say out loud; the artist is probably standing behind you. Chances are he/she is not a kindergartener.

10. Either of the two hardware stores. You can show off your fix-it skills and legitimately use words like "ball pean." In the plumbing section, you can ask for nipples! Talk about testosterone.

If none of these great ideas work and you still find yourself alone and wanting attention, there is only one sure-fire alternative. During any morning commute, attempt to turn north onto Vashon Highway from 112th, but wait for a wide spot in the ferry line that is there because somebody fell asleep in his/her car waiting for the line to move. You'll be butting into the ferry line, which technically is a violation of State law, BUT you'll instantly be the subject of lots of peoples' attention, including the rugged and handsome State Trooper and his cute bomb-sniffing dog! You never know which one will turn out to be your soul mate, and the chances are reasonably good that you won't get a ticket.

Educational Opportunities (you're never too old for things that might prove embarrassing when the paramedics arrive)

ON OUR LITTLE island, there are numerous educational opportunities even for adults who are too old to sneak back into high school, not that I have ever done that. They range from weekly classes given by local non-profit organizations (Vashon Allied Arts, the Land Trust, etc.) to many one-day events given by these same organizations as well as local businesses and island artists. Clearly, there are too many to list here, and they are ephemeral besides, so if I composed a list, it would be obsolete before I could figure out how to spell obsolete. If you are interested in taking a class in something or attending a seminar, look in *The Beachcomber* or check at the Vashon Allied Arts office in the Blue Heron Gallery for available listings of upcoming classes.

Believe it or not, Vashon also has a college. It's not a real college, at least it doesn't seem to be because their web site currently says they have no courses to offer. There are professors listed, but without any actual classes, I'm guessing there aren't any actual students. I had thought that the presence of students was required for most colleges.

Nevertheless, Vashon College has had a remarkable history. Founded in 1892, the college was housed in buildings on the hill above Burton. Apparently, everything went well for about 20 years until there was a disastrous fire and classes were suspended due to lack of a college. And then in 2005, Vashon College was incorporated as a nonprofit and the principals announced, in a fashion reminiscent of the movie *Poltergeist*, "We're back!" Oddly, none of the principals smelled the least bit like smoke.

The absence of formal college classes need not stop the intrepid student from finding many other educational opportunities on Vashon. Even casual visitors discover rather quickly (mostly because there isn't much else to do) that we are awash in educational opportunities even just around the house. Lessons abound in everyday life, and I'm going to list a few such unofficial "classes" for you to ponder. Using the ideas below, you can go to the library, check out a book or two on the appropriate topic, and your class has started.

If you are interested in ranching on Vashon, you can study *Beginning Animal Husbandry*, a survey of common landscaping plants that can be used to raise deer. For the budding farmers out there, you might like *Suburban Horticulture*. Discover the best places to find blackberries before the neighbors get them, and learn ways to kill that ivy that is advancing upon your property from the neighbor's back yard without being discovered by the neighbor. There is a lab with this class that meets at the hardware store in the herbicide section.

Dying to learn about human interactions in small-town America? There's *Socialization in a Community Context*, where you can observe interactions within several age groups. Park yourself in front of Thriftway and meet lots of people, or observe Geezer mating rituals during First Friday Gallery Cruises and get a free glass of wine to boot. For teens, you can observe pubescent behavior at *Late Nights at the Library*. Take your camera to both places, because you might be able to capture the flashes of green light that are attributed by some to hormone bursts.

But you don't even need to leave the house to learn many of life's lessons, chemistry and physics among them. All you have to do is hang out in the kitchen.

When I got into college, I learned that there are two categories of chemistry: "Organic" and "Inorganic." Prior to that, I had already discovered that there are two categories through trial and error (mostly error), but the two categories I had identified were "Harmless Household Chemistry of the Kind You Learn About in Science Class" and "Serious Chemistry of the Kind You Learn About After Taking Firecrackers Apart." To be truly helpful in life, you only need to know about the Household kind, but if you're a boy, at some point you'll ask older males about the Serious kind. It's kind of like learning about "the birds and the bees," but with the added potential of abruptly losing small body parts.

Household chemistry comes in really handy from time to time. For instance, my father used to call water "the universal solvent." I never could figure out why, but I assumed that he meant that if you left something in water for long enough, it would dissolve.

When I got out on my own, I reasoned that if I left the dishes soaking in the sink long enough, all of that grease and burned-on cheese would melt away. It does actually work that way, particularly if you add a little detergent to make the water wetter. How long you can leave the dishes in the sink usually correlates with how convincing you can appear to the spouse. For me, it works for about 90 minutes.

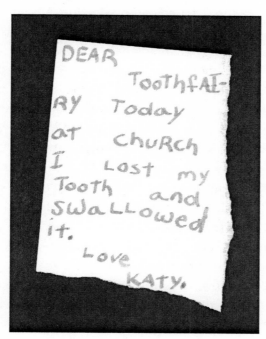

If you were to study nutrition, you would learn that swallowing teeth may be beneficial to your health, provided you need some serious roughage.

Kitchen chemistry also includes cooking chemistry. You can get a primer of what is in the food you eat simply by reading the ingredient lists on the packages. Some lists (such as for bread) are simple and generally understandable. Others (including most junk foods) require an advanced degree in organic toxicology. It is better not to read those complicated lists after dinner time, because you might be kept awake at night. If you've actually eaten the contained junk food, it will be even worse.

For instance, you will discover that soda pop contains acid. Yes, it actually does contain acid, and enough acid to dissolve rocks. I'm not kidding about that. Soda pop contains carbonic acid that will dissolve the calcite in limestone. I used to amaze adults when I was eight years old (it didn't take much back then) by dropping a piece of limestone into some 7^{up} and watching it effervesce as the acid attacked the calcite and released carbon dioxide. Any soda would have worked; I used the 7^{up} because it was clear. Some sodas also contain phosphoric acid, which can dissolve the same mineral that makes up your teeth (calcium phosphate). Oddly, none of the adults stopped me from drinking soda pop, nor did they stop drinking it themselves. But then again, you can't make a rum and Coke without some collateral damage. Losing a few teeth may be the least of your worries.

And speaking of losing things, whatever happened to the missing vitamins? We all know about A, B (1 to 12), C, D, E, and K. What happened to F, G, H, I, and J? Are we to assume that there are no vitamins at all above K? Should we instead assume that vitamin scientists don't know the alphabet? These questions have puzzled me for a long time, and will continue to do so until I look up the answers.

But getting back to soda pop, there are two good uses for soda pop that can be approved by even the most cautious science teacher. One of them I can't write about here because this book is intended to be G-rated. The other, of course, involves Mentos.

If you are not currently a middle-schooler, you may be unaware that by dropping an entire roll of Mentos into a quart bottle of soda pop, you will create an erupting volcano of sticky mint-flavored liquid that erupts out of the plastic bottle with a force similar to that exhibited by Mt. St. Helens. That is, you will be able to do that if you can get the entire roll of mints into the container of soda rapidly. If you're slow or lose a few to the outside of the bottle, your eruption will be less impressive, and this happens most of the time because it's danged hard to get all the mints into the bottle quickly.

Recently, I funded a series of Mentos-In-Soda experiments undertaken (purely out of scientific curiosity) by my wife's youngest child, Marie, and Marie's friend, Tasha. They went through probably 15 quart bottles of soda and an even larger number of rolls of Mentos (taste testing was part of the experiment) to find that diet sodas react roughly the same as non-diet sodas. It took about three good rainstorms to get all the sugar out of the grass in the back yard, and the girls got so soaked with soda pop that they literally stuck to anything they brushed against. We had to hose them off outside after peeling them off the deck where they sat down for a rest.

The explosive nature of junk foods as described above might be a good transition into a discussion about Serious Chemistry. Before we get too deeply into that, it might be good to lay the groundwork with a brief explanation of the Periodic Table.

For those of you who never took a science class, or live in a cave, the Periodic Table is a big chart of all the elements arranged by atomic number. The atomic number is the number of protons in the nucleus of the atom. The Periodic Table was invented in 1869 by a Russian chemist, Dmitri Mendeleev, who later lost his eyesight from trying to count so many tiny protons.

If I hadn't been taught that a Russian invented the Table, I'd have guessed it anyway because Russians love to classify things in huge schemes, but the truth of the matter is that a number of Europeans were making up classification schemes for the elements beginning in the 1700s. The first one was pretty simple, having only Fire, Water, Air, and Earth in a chart with four boxes.

Back when Mendeleev made up his table, there were many fewer elements than there are today, mainly because lots of elements don't occur as pure or "native" elements in nature, but rather you find them mixed with other elements so that they all look like earth, water, or air. By the time I got into college, there were about 103 elements known. Now, there are officially 114, of which those with atomic numbers 95 and above are "manufactured," meaning they were experimentally made by scientists who like to smash things together in the Superconducting Supercollider.

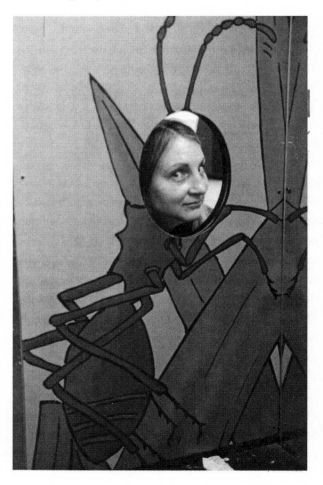

This woman took a class on how to communicate with common insects, and discovered that it also helped her talk to my Aunt Bea.

The first elements were named in antiquity, probably by Romans since their names have Latin roots. Lead, for instance, is plumbum in Latin, hence the symbol Pb, and hence the profession "plumbers." Gold was aurum (Au...an easy way to remember this, if you're a James Bond fan, is to think of Auric Goldfinger), silver was argentum (Ag), and copper was cuprum (Cu). But since then, naming the new elements has gotten to be a bit of a circus. Apparently, we've run out of normal names, and so the scientists who have discovered the newest elements have resorted to names like ununtrium (113), ununquadium (114), and ununpentium (115). I have to conclude that these scientists have somehow gotten their ties caught in the Superconducting Supercollider, or perhaps they've been sniffing fumes from their plastic pocket protectors. They refer to regular names (like oxygen and sulfur) as "trivial" names...and bemoan the fact that they can't think of any. Why didn't they ask a geologist, is my question.

I've gotten a little off-track, but now you can understand why the chemical formula for common table salt (sodium chloride) is NaCl. Na is sodium (natron in Latin) and Cl is chlorine (chlorine in Latin). Sodium chloride is what makes sea water salty. It is what you taste if you kiss your lover on the neck after he/she's been exercising. It is also what you sprinkle in your beer (if you're a redneck), put on green onions (if you eat green onions raw), and brush off your shirt if you have been eating a lot of potato chips. Together, sodium and chlorine combine to make a compound that is as important to your body as water. Your blood contains a LOT of it, even more if you live in the Midwest or South.

But pry those two elements apart, and you have both a fiery explosive and a deadly poison! Think of that....we eat these things every day never knowing we might explode in a cloud of poisonous gas! Okay, I'm exaggerating a bit, but you never know.

I actually had some real sodium metal once. When I was in high school, there was an advertisement in the paper for a garage sale at a private chemistry lab. "*Glassware, instruments, and chemicals, all need to be sold,*" declared the classified ad. I was in heaven. I called some friends of mine, and we all drove to the sale in my 1959 Edsel Ranger.

My 1959 Edsel Ranger.

This guy had an amazing lab, and all of his stuff was for sale. Everything! We bought glassware, thermometers, Ph papers, and chemicals, too. I got 20 pounds of liquid mercury (which should have worried my parents, had they known) that I sold on the way home to a scrap metal dealer. I pocketed a profit of $35, a fortune in 1969.

I also snagged a bottle of sodium metal cubes kept in kerosene, at least a pound of real sodium metal! Sodium metal oxidizes rapidly when exposed to air, so it is commonly kept in kerosene. Until that day, I had only dreamt of having any sodium metal, and here I had a whole bottle of it! Right in my hands! So I took it home, put it on the shelf in the basement, and there it sat for the better part of five years.

Sodium metal is not like other metals you know. It's more like silvery cold butter, and you can actually cut it with a knife. When you drop sodium metal into water, it instantly reacts with the water to make hydrogen gas and sodium hydroxide, which is the same stuff you use to unclog drains. The reaction is so rapid and exothermic (heat generating) that the hydrogen instantly burns.

Eventually, I realized that I had no use for sodium metal, and the lid on the jar was getting a bit rusty, so I took it back to where I was going to college in central Missouri. One winter day, I drove out to a secluded spot on the Little Piney River. I wandered up the river and found a quiet eddy into which I dropped a cube of sodium, anxious to see what would happen. The metal instantly popped up in fragments, each fizzing and hissing on the surface of the water as hydrogen was being generated. There were little popping fireballs everywhere, each exploding and scattering smaller fireballs until they were all gone.

With a screwdriver, I poked some holes into the lid of the jar containing the rest of the sodium, poured out the kerosene, and added a few rocks. I lobbed the jar into a deep pool at the river's edge. It sank slowly, with a few bubbles coming out of the holes. Suddenly, there where more bubbles...and then WHOOOM.

Have you ever seen one of those war movies where the Navy is dropping depth charges to kill an enemy submarine? It was just like that. The surface of the river bulged in a mass of bubbles as a shock wave lifted the ground on which I was standing. A huge mass of tiny sodium fragments spread across the water, each flaming and hissing. And then all was quiet.

I may have irritated a few fish that day. In my defense, I felt I was returning balance to the universe by disposing of the unstable sodium. The small amount of resulting sodium hydroxide was instantly diluted and washed away, and the hydrogen burned to recreate water. But there have been other times and other experiments that were not so harmless. If I write about them here, I may be getting a call from the Department of Homeland Security.

Suffice it to say that such dangerous experiments cannot be done by teenagers today, and praise be to the gods for that! In 1969, you could order by mail an incredible selection of dangerous chemicals without any questions whatsoever. Now, you'd be lucky if you could purchase any sodium chloride that way. In 1969, you could also walk into any drug store and purchase the ingredients to make gunpowder. Nowadays, I can't even get a cold medicine that works.

So, parents, fear not as my parents did that your child will create a contact explosive that damages the ping pong table, or a compound that burns through manhole covers. Don't worry about finding pipe fragments in the back yard that look like they went through atmospheric reentry. Your kids are a lot safer and better behaved today, except maybe for the drugs and sex and availability of handguns.

As awkward as this transition is, I have to say that when I think of handguns, I think of balistics and trajectories. When I think of balistics and trajectories, I think of physics class.

Physics class was always tough for me, both in high school and college, because there are lots of numbers you have to memorize and some of them are quite puzzling. What is even more puzzling is how the guys who invented these numbers ever came up with them. I mean, really, how could anyone have ever discovered the value for π?

π (the Greek letter, or Pi in Latin characters), is an irrational number, meaning that its value cannot be expressed exactly as a fraction m/n, where m and n are integers. Consequently, its decimal representation never ends or repeats. Its value is a string of never-ending unrepeating numbers, none of which the average person can predict. But just for reference, it's 3.141592653589andfromthereyou'reonyourown.

How the π Guy ever discovered it was beyond me until I learned that π is simply a mathematical constant whose value is the ratio of any circle's circumference to its diameter *in Euclidean space*. I'm not sure why Euclidean space is any different from Everyday space, but if you mistakenly leave off those last three words from the definition, it makes more sense.

So all you have to do is divide the circumference by the diameter of any circle anywhere you see one! How easy is that?!? Some ancient guy simply watched a horse cart go by and kept his eye on the wheel moving and the track it was making on the ground, and it came to him in a big Duh moment. Later, Archimedes or someone like him discovered that π is also the value of the ratio of a circle's area to the square of its radius. And lots of other guys used it from that day forward, making up formulae in science and engineering that plague us to this day.

I'm guessing (or rather hypothesizing) that all the other numbers we had to memorize (Planck's Constant, Avogadro's Number, absolute zero, etc) and all those confusing laws (Boyle's Law, Charles' Law, the Heisenberg Uncertainty Principle, etc) started out the same way. Somebody made a simple observation that simply got out of hand, sort of like what happens between the time something actually happens and the moment it's reported on the Evening News.

Some of these numbers and equations do have value, and here I am thinking of one I learned in college that has proven to be far more valuable than any other. It is Avocado's Number: the number of small tomatoes you will need to dice with one small onion and one regular avocado to the make the Perfect Guacamole. After learning it, I wrote it on a small piece of paper that I kept in my wallet for years. Few people know this number, and so my guacamole became famous far and wide. Combined with the Perfect Margarita (there's a formula for one that requires you to solve a differential equation), the Perfect Guacamole can bring you health, wealth, and infinite power over people of the opposite sex.

Just for fun, I've hidden Avocado's Number somewhere in the text of this book. When you find it, let me know, because my wallet went through the laundry this morning.

Religion on Vashon (inside church and out)

IF YOU HAPPEN to be on Vashon for more than a day or two, or you're really into going to church, you might find yourself searching for a house of worship. Real guidebooks might give you only a list of local churches and times of worship, without any warnings or recommendations like "They serve real wine for communion," or "Whatever you do, don't ask the vicar if he can play the guitar."

It's not my job to steer you towards or away from a particular church, and if you want a list of them, just grab a phone book. Churches are found between "Chiropractors" and "Civil Engineers," which seems oddly appropriate.

About all I can do in this regard is to assure you that no matter what your preference, we've got every species of religion known to man on this little island, and then some. Our religious venues range from the conventionally conservative through the moderate and all the way down to the totally whacked out and strange. We even have a monastery where there are monks with long beards and long robes, like the kind you would expect friars to wear, and I don't mean small chickens. Given that wide diversity, you'd think that some groups might be intolerant of others and out to get them. But tolerance is something we've got in spades.

In the time I've lived here, there have been senseless acts of vandalism directed at four different churches. The Havurat was broken into and vandalized (presumably by teenagers), the Catholic church was vandalized and its safe stolen, the Presbyterian church had their stained glass window smashed by a homeless man, and the Mormon church was burglarized and the wooden doors damaged during a summer of burglaries that outraged the public and had us wondering if the Sheriff did anything but eat donuts.

Political activism is a form of religion to many people on Vashon.

Each time, the community rose in support of these churches. When the Havurat was vandalized, the public support included rallies in the center of town. When St. John's safe went missing, islanders mounted a treasure hunt and eventually found it off the end of the Tramp Harbor pier. And the shattered window of the Presbyterian church was painstakingly restored by a talented island artist with support from many community members.

My point is that we accept everyone here. We don't criticize or make fun of each other based on religious beliefs. Instead make fun of political outliers, including aging hippies (which is all good-natured fun because many of us ARE aging hippies), Republicans, Tea Party advocates, and other flat-Earthers. This also includes folks who oppose Darwin and his radical "theory" of the evolution of man.

Oddly, if evolution was restricted to non-human beings, I doubt even the religious right would have a problem with it. Everyone accepts that you can breed dogs, farm animals, and farm crops. What would we do today if someone hadn't bred maize from its tiny prehistoric ancestor? And aren't new diseases evolving for which we have no effective antibiotics? But there are lots of people, including some very educated ones, who can ignore the evolution going on around them and deny its existence.

When I was in college in Missouri, I had to have my wisdom teeth taken out. I carefully surveyed the available dentists, picked the one who seemed to be the most enlightened (by virtue of his yellow pages ad), and made an appointment. Fortunately, he also happened to be the dentist who was about three blocks from my apartment, so I walked over.

It was while I was sitting in his waiting room that I discovered I might have made a mistake. In place of the standard rack of magazines was a display of literature that claimed evolution was a myth. Darwin was an evil apostate and possibly a communist, and he was spreading dangerous thoughts that undermined the Kingdom of Heaven and Life Everlasting, according to the tracts.

Referring to the fossil record, the dentist's creation literature appeared to accept the geologic principle of the Law of Superposition, which says that rocks deposited on top of others are therefore younger. The oldest stuff is at the bottom, sort of like the dishes in your sink, and the youngest stuff is on top. This is the primary way that geologists assign relative dates to sedimentary rocks and their enclosed fossils, thus leading to the "theory" of evolution. The creationists accepted this primary rule, but then ignored the fact that sedimentary rocks represent better than one billion years of history. Making the assumption that all sedimentary rocks were created at the same time, they stated that the only reason that trilobites are found in rocks *below* those containing dinosaur fossils is that they could not run as fast from the rising waters of the Great Flood. I was puzzled as to why trilobites, which were marine organisms, would want to run from rising waters anyway, but I decided not to ask my dentist until after my wisdom teeth were safely in his metal tray.

The great thing about this dentist was that he used laughing gas. This was the only time in my life (so far) that I experienced nitrous oxide, which isn't so much laughing gas as it is really-really-relaxing gas. It's like having one-to-many beers and being picked up by a big hand. I asked him if I could get a tank of that gas for party weekends, but being the licensed doctor he was, he told me that would not be technically legal.

It wasn't until the following Sunday morning that I sensed a problem. One of the gaps that used to be a tooth began bleeding like crazy. I called the dentist, but he was apparently at church, so instead I had to phone a godless dentist across town who was sinfully staying home. He told me to suck on a teabag because tea is an astringent.

One thing you should remember is to never bite down on a teabag that you are sucking. You can't help but swallow a lot of tea leaves, and combined with blood they do not sit well in your stomach. I won't tell you what happened next, but it wasn't long before I had lost enough blood that I was getting sleepy. I asked my girlfriend (who happened to be living there on an emergency basis only) to call me a taxi so that I could get to the godless dentist. Always the fun lover, she said "Sure... you're a Taxi."

Eventually I did get to the sinful dentist, and he scraped out my socket with a tiny hoe. I have to say that was the single most unpleasant medical procedure I have ever endured. I felt every scrape deep inside my jaw, and I concurrently learned why everyone hates dentists, especially the two I visited.

I also learned another valuable lesson: if my ancestors hadn't evolved so far, I never would have had problems with my wisdom teeth. My ancestors (I'm thinking of one uncle in particular) had big mouths with huge teeth for eating things that were tough. As humans progressed and became more "gracile," they started eating softer and smaller things, and they could get along with smaller mouths. This may have also been because they invented language and didn't have to grunt and scream so much when it was time to get the kids to clean their rooms, but that's just my theory.

All of these changes to the human mouth occurred in very small steps over a long time. Unfortunately, the number of teeth stayed the same throughout, and eventually the mouth was too small for the teeth. This is sort of like how it is when you slowly gain weight over a period of years and wake up one morning to find that your pants no longer fit.

Evolution is like that, lots of tiny changes over a very long time. Imagine for a moment how that might work. Let's take the example of human stature. It is known that humans in the 1500s were about five inches shorter, on average, than today. That's about one inch of gained height per century, mainly because of better nutrition and government-mandated health care. With the passage of "Obama Care" and the rise of the local food movement, we can assume that this trend will continue indefinitely. This means that in a mere 4000 years, which is about the same amount of time that has passed since the pyramids of Egypt were built, humans will be on average about ten feet tall. We will look like Avatars....only not so blue.

The fossil record only captures a few of those many changes. It's as if your uncle the photographer (not the one with the big mouth) took millions of photos during his career, but you find only three negatives at the estate sale.

Simply stated, the geologic process of fossil preservation is fickle and inconstant. Millions of years can pass without any fossils being preserved, or at least preserved where we can find them easily. You have to find a lot of fossils, over a long period of time and through many paleontologists' careers, to build a database of fossil finds that you can use to sort out the past. All I can say is thank goodness for libraries, because if it wasn't for good record keeping, our past discoveries would be lost and we'd be starting over again and again.

Think what might happen if five million years from now, when humans are about 4200 feet tall (and presumably still not blue), our descendents lost their library card and then found only three fossils of humanoids: some chimpanzees who were trapped in a zoo fire, a handful of adults who perished in a plane crash, and two young people who were waiting in a dentist's office when a landslide hit the building. They might conclude that the only humanoids who had problems with their wisdom teeth were the ones who visited dentists.

Come to think of it, the only time I had a problem with my wisdom teeth was when I was around a dentist. And I wouldn't have had a problem with my wisdom teeth had it not been for evolution. I wonder why God invented it?

This temple cost a fortune in aurum, but most of us on Vashon don't worship the Roman gods. Personally, I'm a fan of Venus. Mars and Jupiter can go suck eggs.

How to Live on Vashon (repent!)

THERE ARE MORE than a few people on Vashon who would like to tell you how to live your life. If you thought your parents were tough, just attend any Community Council meeting and you'll see what I mean. Thankfully, we don't have to rely on normal humans to tell us how to live our lives well and happy on this island. Instead, we can defer to a recent discovery that was made in a new translation of an unabridged copy of the *Book of Exodus*:

"And lo the Honorary Mayor spake these words, saying: "I am thy faux leader, who raised the most money for my favorite charity, who brought ye chosen people out of the land of Seattle, out of the house that had a valid building permit. Observe what I commandst of ye today, or lo, I will drive before ye the Ammonites and the Trilobites, lest ye observe these ten commands:

1. Thou shalt have no other island before ours.
2. Thou shalt not make for thyself any carved image, or any likeness of anything that is in heaven above, or that is in the earth beneath, or that is in the water under the earth, that is not funky and brightly colored. For I, the Mayor of the island of the chosen people, will visit the iniquity of the fathers on those who paint their houses beige and upon those who make their properties look like suburbia, but will show mercy to those who bring an artsy flair to life.

3. Thou shalt not take the name of the island in vain on a regular basis, but once in a while is okay.

4. Remember the Vashon-Maury Island Community Council meeting day and keep it holy. Six days shalt thou labor that week, and do all thy trivial work, but the Council meeting day is like the Sabbath of the Lord thy God. In it thou shalt not make an Ass of thyself by presenting Lame Resolutions or droning on and on about things of which thou knowst nothing. For in six days the Lord made the heavens and the earth, the sea, and all that is in them. On the seventh day, He met with the Galilee Community Council and passed the first resolution, on Dead Sea ferry schedules, and so shouldst thou.

5. Honor thy Building Department and thy Health Department, so that thy days may be long upon the land on which thou wish to build a house.

6. Thou shalt not move the Library.

7. Thou shalt not buy food at a fast food franchise.

8. Thou shalt not steal good art project ideas from other island artists; but for the heathens who do not live on the island, thou shalt smite them and taketh their ideas, for only the chosen shall inherit the Gallery Space.

9. Thou shalt pick up thy dog's poop on KVI Beach unless it is below ordinary high tide, for that is an abomination upon heaven.

10. Thou shalt not covet thy neighbor's house even if it is on the beach, remembering that his septic system likely doth spew odor and pestilence; thou shalt not covet thy neighbor's place in the ferry line, nor his organic vegetable garden, nor his forest management plan, nor his table at your favorite restaurant, nor his llama, nor his brightly painted tractor, nor anything that is thy neighbor's.

Thus spake the Honorary Mayor.

Hints on Buying Property (how to recognize a landslide before it recognizes you)

LIVING ON AN island in Puget Sound is positively magical. Those visitors who first visit in the summer fall in love with the gentle filtered sunlight and the pastel vistas. Almost without exception, they dream of living the island life year-round. This idyllic feeling typically lasts until about a month after the winter rains start, because what long-term residents fail to explain is that "magical" technically includes "turned into a frog."

Water is the most common chemical compound in the Pacific Northwest, being even more prevalent than caffeine, as impossible as that sounds. The presence of water is also an important issue to consider when thinking of buying or building a home. Whether it be from where you get your drinking water (*hopefully, not from a stream*), or where you deposit your waste (*hopefully, not in a stream*), or where you position your residence (*hopefully, not anywhere near a stream*), it's ALL about water. Water is both essential for life and the homeowner's enemy.

There are two types of residential properties that interest people the most: properties with houses at the tops of bluffs (where the views are amazing), and properties with residences near the water (often at the bases of bluffs). These preferences are also recognized by the King County Assessor, who values view and waterfront properties higher than others, whether or not they have approved water supplies or functional septic systems. Besides public interest and high assessments, these two types of properties share a third characteristic: the tendency to be within a landslide hazard area.

This is a house that was destroyed during the Nisqually earthquake of 2001 by a landslide that was triggered by the quake. The sole occupant barely got out the front door as mud was coming in the back. This house was not located on Vashon, but lots of homes and vacation cabins on Vashon have been destroyed in a similar fashion.

Before I say much more about landslides, I need to backtrack a bit and review one of my favorite topics, the Scientific Method. I could make a joke here and assure you that there is Method in my madness. Instead, I ask you to trust me and just keep reading.

For those of you who have forgotten the Scientific Method, I have my *Encyclopedia Britannica* right here, which says that *"Scientific method refers to a body of techniques for investigating phenomena, acquiring new knowledge, or correcting and integrating previous knowledge. To be termed scientific, a method of inquiry must be based on gathering observable, empirical and measurable evidence subject to specific principles of reasoning. A scientific method consists of the collection of data through observation and experimentation, and the formulation and testing of hypotheses."* Is that cool, or what? And not only that, it's what you'll be doing when you look for a home to buy.

This is how you "do" the Scientific Method: first, you pose a question. For example: *Did your teenager sneak out last night?* Next, you invent a way to gather data, or make observations designed to answer the question. *Are his shoes muddy? Are his pants muddy? Did he even wear any pants?* From the accumulated data and observations, you formulate a hypothesis. *He snuck out about midnight to...well, let's skip that part.* Ideally, you then test the hypothesis. *You search his bedroom for...evidence.* The skeptics among you might point out that it would have been a whole lot easier to ask the teenager where he was about 1 AM this morning without any pants. But if you were a scientist like me, you'd already know (because you had already tested that theory) that teenagers do not communicate with human beings. You'd have better luck talking to a Douglas Fir, and the Fir would needle you less.

Using the same method, you can do a preliminary assessment of whether or not there is a landslide hazard (which is the question you are posing) by gathering data and making observations. You can use the following list of data-gathering questions to guide your efforts:

1. Has any portion of the yard or house mysteriously disappeared in years past?
2. Have any new yard areas or structures appeared spontaneously, especially after a hard rain?
3. Can you find any cracks in the ground, especially near the top of a steep slope, in which you can insert your finger?
4. Can you find any cracks in the ground in which you could insert a Buick Riviera?
5. Is there any part of the house, including the foundation, that doesn't seem to line up with adjoining parts?
6. Has anyone been killed here or on adjacent properties by rapidly moving soil?

If you can answer yes to any of these questions, you should at the very least wear a hard hat and some good running shoes the next time you visit the property. If you're near the water, you might also want to keep a personal flotation device nearby. And finally, as a matter of liability avoidance, I need to tell you to hire a professional geological engineer or engineering geologist and find out if there really is a problem, because things aren't often as bad as I've made them sound. On the other hand, sometimes things are worse. Most landslide hazards go unrecognized until it's too late, sort of like the way jerky in-laws appear after a wedding. If you don't want your neighbor's mud, or your spouse's uncle, to show up in your bedroom in the middle of the night, you might want to get ahead of the situation.

And speaking of heads (as they are called in the Navy), another thing to worry about if you are in the market for a property on Vashon is the status of the septic system. Those of you who have lived in cities or suburbs all your life may not know about septic systems, so a little explanation is in order. *Warning:* You might not want to read this next part while you are eating.

In town, when you flush a toilet, everything goes into a pipe (a sanitary sewer) and is taken to a treatment plant where all that mess is somehow miraculously transformed into water so clean you can drink it. At least that's what they claim. You don't see the Directors of the Sewer District drinking that water.

In the country, there are no sanitary sewers. Instead, when you flush a toilet, all that mess goes out into your backyard where it enters a tank (that captures the big chunks), and then into a system of perforated pipes that allows the fluids to trickle slowly into the soil just below your grass. With luck, the mess will stay below your grass. Bacteria in the soil eat the nastier parts, leaving water so clean you can drink it. At least that's what they claim.

But onsite sewage systems, as they are formally called, aren't designed to last forever, and when they fail, they can fail big-time. Until they do, they require periodic maintenance. The tank needs to be pumped out roughly every three years, sooner if your kindergartener has been flushing fruit or small toys, as I have known some to do. Unless you want to step out into your backyard some morning and sink up to your knees in "fertilizer," you have to keep up with the maintenance. Having an onsite sewage system is like buying a home with a barn and finding a live elephant in the barn when you move in. They eat a lot, and there are big messes to clean up.

Popularly known as septic systems, most homes on Vashon have one. Many of these work properly, at least as far as we know. Other homes may discharge directly to Puget Sound (particularly those on the water) or have bootlegged systems that cannot be sanctioned by the Health Department. Non-functioning or non-existent septic systems are so common that all home buyers are urged to inquire as to the status of the septic system before looking further at a house. In fact, it's now the law that all onsite sewage systems have to be inspected prior to selling a house. Hopefully, the inspection result won't be "none," because new systems can cost a few dimes. Roughly 300,000 dimes.

Even with landslides and water problems, life on Vashon Island can be beautiful and exciting. With the right partner to help watch for dangers, you can be warm, dry, and free of trouble most of the time. I married Margaret precisely for this reason. She is beautiful, exciting, and she has a tight roof, a smart structure, a solid foundation, and would be approved by the Health Department if anyone thought to ask. She is my home. The house is just a house.

Making Life Work Once You Live Here (guidelines you'll never follow)

PEOPLE ON VASHON live pretty much the same way people every-where else do, but with fewer stylish clothes and building permits. We go through the same stages of life and experience the same joys and disappointments, perhaps more so when it comes to politics.

Vashonistas know they are part of this bigger picture of society, but perhaps out of self defense we try to maintain the illusion that we are somehow different from the rest of the people in King County. Not special, just different. "Keep Vashon Weird" says the bumper sticker. The problem with this is that I've seen "Keep (your town here) Weird" bumper stickers in Austin (TX), Boulder (CO), Taos (NM), Bozeman (MT), and Bisbee (AZ). I'm guessing that there's a company that does nothing but print personalized bumper stickers for just about every small town in America that is feeling overwhelmed by an expanding suburbia and simultaneously pushed into conformity by the media and the internet. We're all starting to look like a standard strip mall, and some of us don't like it.

Another thing that unites us all, besides a desire to actually buy some-thing at Restoration Hardware, is dying. As you might guess, a number of scientists have spent large amounts of grant money investigating what some think is the greatest mystery: what happens when we die.

Personally, I think the greatest mystery we face is why the French seem to have all the fashion genes for our species. I went to Paris once and spent an entire day walking around in my best suit, just purchased at a posh store in Denver specifically for that trip. Nevertheless, I felt the whole time like I was wearing flip-flops, shorts decorated with chili peppers, and a Colorado Rockies baseball cap on sideways. It wasn't until a month after I came back from Paris that I could look at my countrymen without feeling sorry for them.

And although I wanted to die of embarrassment in Paris, I didn't want to die so much as to be in a scientific experiment. Some people have literally died for science, usually when they didn't know they were involved. But a few have consented to have lots of measurements taken when they expired, an action that in those cases we must assume was unpreventable. The amazing thing is that some of these studies have shown there is a small change in body weight upon dying that cannot be explained. Some folks immediately assume it is the weight of the soul. I think it just as easily could be the weight that is lifted off your shoulders when you realize you no longer have to go into the office on Monday.

Theologians tell us that "the wages of sin is death." Scientists counter with "the wages of sex is death." What the scientists mean is that for life forms that reproduce sexually, evolution can only work, and life can only survive in the hostile environments of the future, if all individuals grow old and die. Basically, the cost of having sex is death. Being a good parent, I tried to instill this belief in my children when they were teenagers, but to no avail.

Sex and death are intricately interwoven in the fabric of our being. Indeed, every stage of life has aspects of both. So without further ado, I want to share my view of the stages of life, which are purposely offered without age boundaries. That is because some folks pass through these stages faster than others. For instance, lots of people in Texas never get past Stage Three before they run out of play time. These are "young souls," some folks might say.

1. Birth: We're assuming one per person, but there may be more depending upon whether you believe in reincarnation. Anyway, it's our starting point for the stages of life.
2. The Growing Stage: This stage is characterized by rapid body growth and a longing to be older. In this stage, you want to

be older so that you can do cool stuff, like have sex and drink beer. It's all about body growth rather than spiritual growth, and the faster the better.

3. The Early Grownup Stage: You're now old enough to have sex and drink beer, not necessarily in that order, but now you're thinking that if you had some money and power, you could get even more sex and beer. Although you're happy, you haven't yet "made it."

4. The Middle Grownup Stage: You're now old enough to have control of your life and most of your thoughts, except those gleaned from the media, and you appreciate good sex and good beer and are thoughtful about the future. You haven't yet seen that train heading toward you.

5. The Hey-Wait-A-Minute Stage: Now you're a little bit too old, or at least your current sexual partner is a little too old, and you're beginning to wonder if you are missing something somewhere else. You start to feel something pulling you backwards. This stage may be quite brief.

6. The "Mature" Grownup Stage: Okay, you're now certain that you're too old and you want to get out of your body and reboot the game. You may make some silly choices and you may break some hearts, including yours, but you can always rationalize silliness with New Age theology. Thank goodness for California, sports cars, and nude sunbathing!

7. The Wise Grownup Stage: Winston Churchill once said that Americans can always be counted on to do the right thing, after they've exhausted all the other possibilities. By now, you've exhausted all of your possibilities, or you're too tired to keep trying. So you sit back and enjoy life like you've never done before, with wisdom and humor and a certain "joie de vivre." You may even visit Paris and feel comfortable wearing a Sears outfit to the Louvre. This great feeling lasts for just a moment, until....

8. Death: See "Birth," above.

If you think those stages go by too quickly, you should remember that there are ways to slow them all down. You can even increase the wisdom quotient of each, although one way or another, you'll have to experience all of the stages. Still, lengthening the time you spend in each may correspond to lengthening your entire life, and a long life is one of the two measures of success for a human. The other is how many children you can claim. You don't have to claim them out loud; this is not like with the Internal Revenue Service.

Which brings me to my next list: *Twenty Things That Age You Prematurely.* Clearly, this is not an exhaustive list, although I was exhausted when I finished it. If you think of other factors that make you feel old and that you'd like to change, write them down and send them in a letter addressed to: *Attn: Things That Need Changing, 1600 Pennsylvania Ave., Washington, DC.* Make it clear in the letter that you want these things fixed, and now!

Twenty Things That Age You Prematurely:

1. Too much food, sex, or exercise.
2. Not enough food, sex, or exercise.
3. Too much cheap red wine.
4. Not enough cheap red wine.
5. Living in the American Midwest or South for more than 14 days.
6. Talking to Republicans or people who don't believe in evolution.
7. Going to family reunions.
8. Listening to the news on anything other than National Public Radio.
9. Teenagers. Anywhere and all the time.
10. Looking in a mirror.
11. Working in an office cubicle.
12. Forgetting the anniversary of your marriage.
13. Forgetting your spouse's birthday.

14. Forgetting where you left the corkscrew.
15. Smoking (tobacco).
16. Looking at a French fashion magazine.
17. Being caught at airport security with more than three ounces of shampoo.
18. Receiving a letter from Selective Service.
19. Receiving a letter from the I.R.S.
20. Receiving a letter from A.A.R.P.

Unfortunately (or fortunately for those of us who like sex), death seems inevitable. At least, it seemed inevitable to me until a few years ago when our society was barraged with zombie movies. There are now zombies everywhere you turn, many of whom live in Bellevue. But Vashon is remarkably free of zombies (political and otherwise), partly I think because we are an older and wiser population, demographically speaking.

A sign possibly observed near Bellevue, Washington. Coincidence? I don't think so.

Years ago, Vashon was populated mainly by farmers, fishermen, and other rural types. During the 60s and 70s, young people moved here to take advantage of the cheap rent, privacy, and marijuana growing capacity of the countryside, and Vashon gained a reputation as a hippie hangout. Since then, the demographic has shifted again in favor of the oldsters, mainly because of growing property values that forced out the young and the restless. But Vashon is still a hotbed of radicalism, if by radicals you mean folks who voted for Obama, are typically over 50, and own more than one home.

I'm guessing that if you live here, or have purchased this book, there's a good chance you are at least middle-aged, on your second marriage or contemplating one, have older kids (who may or may not be yours), with enough disposable income to go out to dinner at least once a week. This would place you in at least Stage Four of the life stages listed above. It would also suggest that what you will need more than anything to keep you and your spouse both positive and entertained during the long wet winters is a list of rules for a happy marriage, Vashon style.

Sixty years ago, James Thurber penned "My Own Ten Rules For A Happy Marriage." One would presume that these rules are still sufficient to allow a husband to avoid a blow on the head with a glass ashtray, so I would not advocate discounting them. But here on Vashon Island, things are a little different. In that spirit, I offer the following *Ten Rules For A Happy Marriage On Vashon Island*:

1. Never disparage your partner's Tibetan prayer flags, scented candles, essential oils, new chain saw, or emergency generator. Even if they make your nose run or your ears hurt. Just smile when asked if you like them and say "They're nice, dear."

2. Never question the need to go "over town" (to Seattle), even if it's only to shop for something your partner has no intention of buying. Everyone needs a day away from the island, and the ferry system can't survive without lots of discretionary trips.

3. Don't even think about avoiding recurring events like the Strawberry Festival, even if last year some snotty kid dumped a plate of strawberry shortcake on your new shoes. When asked if you want to go to wherever it is, just answer, "Yes, that would be nice, dear." If it's Strawberry Festival, remember that there's a beer garden.

4. Never disparage your partner for not wanting to get a building permit. He/she probably knows what he/she's doing. When the new deck collapses during a dinner party, just exclaim that you're glad you have a husband/wife who can fix it.

5. When your spouse's car gets low on gas, fill it up. Don't tell your spouse you filled it up in Seattle and used the savings to pay the ferry fare you incurred in order to go shopping for something your partner thinks is frivolous.

6. When it's your turn to make dinner, never thaw out a frozen mass-produced pizza. Do your stomach a favor and get a decent pizza at The Rock.

7. No matter how many animals there are in your house or who brought them, you have to love them all. When the cat vomits on your bookshelf, just remark "Oh dear, I'll have to clean that up." Remember that someone else can be assigned to clean the litter box.

8. Be happy that you have one theatre, and don't pine for big city entertainment. It's not that great, anyway, unless maybe Diana Krall is performing somewhere.

9. Never worry about where the kids are...they can't have gone too far, unless they stole your ferry pass. Remember that it's only a few years before they leave anyway, and practice makes perfect.

10. Whatever you do, don't do anything else that would offend your independent-minded spouse. I realize this is a rule that is non-specific and ill-defined, but all I'm saying is to just be careful. If you fail in this respect, do the dishes.

Now it may be that my spouse will be reading this. She looked over my shoulder as I was writing part of it (a VERY early first draft, I must say), and rolled her eyes. I trust that when she reads it this time, she will say something like "That's nice, dear."

Things to Consider (debunking Vashon's myths)

THOSE OF US who live on Vashon believe that the island is unique. We feel lucky to be in our refuge of tranquility. I agree that it's nice here, but there are some things we believe about this place that are not accurate. I've catalogued 18. You only get 10 because to reveal all would spoil the surprises that await you. In mystery there is pleasure, n'est pa?

Myth No. 1: There are two islands. There used to be two islands, if by "island" you mean "land surrounded by water *some* of the time." Decades ago, someone with leftover dirt dumped it at Portage (now misnamed) and connected the two, making ONE island. Often we resolve such conflicts by combining the names of the two places, as in Seatac. We could do that here and call the combined islands Vashry. Those who live here would be Vashryites, which sounds vaguely biblical. Or we could give Maury the first-place nod and call it Mauron. I and my neighbors would be Maurons. I like that better, and depending upon who you ask, it may be more accurate.

Myth No. 2: The southern end of the island is poisonous. It is true that decades of air pollution originating from the ASARCO smelter in Tacoma deposited arsenic (and other elements) in soils close to the smelter site or otherwise downwind. Most of the island (except where I live) registers above the state-recommended cleanup concentration, with the highest soil concentrations of arsenic being on Maury Island, around Quartermaster Harbor, on the Burton peninsula, and the rest of Vashon south of Burton. No studies have identified any impact on public health from the arsenic, and the reason is simple: not many people eat dirt. If you live on Vashon, you should keep your kids from eating the soil, but an adult would have to eat a lot of dirt to get a significant dose. In my opinion, that would take way more ketchup than a person could ever afford.

Myth No. 3: Our woodlands are pristine. Yeah, right. As explained in a previous chapter, the island was logged more than once with no forest management, and invasive plants have taken over. If you want to help restore our woodlands, adopt the mantra "Kill The Ivy." Buy a machete and repeat the mantra while standing in your front yard. Demonstrate your *Weed Warrior Pose* for tourists. You might gain fame among Yoga enthusiasts and find a new career as a featured news item.

Myth No. 4: We are more independent than the rest of King County. It's true that we are pretty independent, but if you go off-island, you'll discover that the folks in eastern King County border on downright scary. They are so independent that they vote Republican. "Going Rogue" for them can include sex with farm animals. Think about that the next time you leave Vashon.

Myth No. 5: We are more environmentally conscious than most people. It may be that we think about the environment more, but we also have more time to think while we are sitting in our cars on the diesel-burning ferry. Some people here think the best thing we can do for the environment is to kill the deer. Personally, I think we need to go after raccoons. With raccoons, it's either them or me.

Myth No. 6: Dogs pooping on the beach is the reason Quartermaster Harbor is contaminated. I'm a supporter of canines but not so big a one as to hide a dog poop problem. I don't think I've seen a dog on the beach in Quartermaster Harbor, but those houses are nice. I guess they are pricey because every one has a top-of-the-line septic system. I haven't a clue why Quartermaster Harbor is contaminated, but the dogs aren't to blame. Maybe those otters have something to do with it.

Myth No. 7: Tofu is an aphrodisiac. It has been my experience (wink, wink) that this only works when you use a special marinade, the recipe for which I cannot divulge without receiving $5 for "reproduction" costs. I cannot guarantee success. Individual results may vary, but man oh man, there was this one night last April....

Myth No. 8: Those noisy boats on July 4th are part of Vashon's treasured heritage. Yes, just as backfiring cars are revered in Chicago, and coal mine explosions are the crown jewel of Appalachia. I recognize there are people here who love annoying things, and my hat is knocked off to them, but every July 4th I pay homage to the earplug.

Myth No. 9: UFOs are sighted here every night. It has been weeks since I've seen an alien being, but others may have better luck. My friend the Sheriff's deputy says he sees unidentified flying objects every night coming out of the bars at closing time.

Myth No. 10: We can be self-sufficient if we want. Actually, this may be true. We may be able to grow enough trees for both firewood and lumber, and we can make wine from blackberries. For meat, I suggest we develop a taste for venison, or better yet raccoon. I'm off now to make an arrowhead. I wonder where I can buy some flint?

Unreal Things to See or Listen For (some of which you may prefer to avoid)

IF YOU GET tired of seeing the same sights that all the other tourists view, I suggest you wander "off the beaten path" and discover some of the unusual (and occasionally mythical) places and things that can be found, and sometimes lost again, on Vashon. This includes sounds as well as sights, and the most famous sound is the Vashon Hum.

The Vashon Hum was first mentioned in *The Beachcomber* during 2010, and it became famous to the point of being mentioned on Seattle news programs. I'm guessing that *The Beachcomber* ran their original story because it was somewhat humorous and a space filler for a slow news week. Consequently, we didn't expect the networks to pick up the story, reasoning that real news would be held in higher regard. We were proven wrong about that. Still, it was fun and several islanders were interviewed on television, including one who owes me because I directed the reporter to him.

As described by most people, the Vashon Hum is a low frequency hum that you can hear if everything else is very quiet, such as in the middle of the night when you can't sleep. Only a little background noise can drown it out, so you have to be in a very very quiet spot to hear it.

You might guess that there are more than a few theories regarding the origin of the Hum, and you'd be right. To date, no one has identified the source. To be honest, no one has proven the Hum even exists, despite some attempts utilizing high-tech audio equipment. Nevertheless, that hasn't stopped many people from believing in the Hum.

Most people postulate that the Hum is just background industrial noise from our surrounding urban areas, such as traffic noise or maybe motor noise from passing ships. But you can hear it no matter where you are on the island. It's no louder near Seattle.

I separate the possible causes into two categories: *Natural* and *Manmade*. I include as *Natural* those that originate with humans but are not intentional (such as industrial background noise). Sources of noise like Rap music and Sarah Palin clearly fall into the *Manmade* category (subcategory *Irritating Whines*).

Natural causes also include those sounds made by extraterrestrials, but I do not list them here because it has been weeks since I've seen one. And unlike many on the island, I do not find the presence of large subterranean worms credible, despite the discovery of huge burrows on the west side. There are plenty of other potential natural causes; some that I wish to list include:

1. Cosmic radiation: We all know that our Sun emits massive amounts of radiation, which in space would fry us like corn dogs. "The atmosphere is our friend," but as the atmosphere warms because of carbon dioxide, it also thins, and more radiation reaches the Earth's surface, causing changes to the soil and rocks. This could include aural effects, particularly just before critical thinning is reached and we cook in a natural microwave oven. Try not to think about this.

2. Mentioned by others was low frequency waves used in marine communication, but there are also low frequency sounds that emanate from seismic zones. All those rocks grinding against each other make a low rumble, and here we are sitting on top of a convergent margin. Duh.

3. Another geologic source could be because we are pumping ground water at rates never before seen (everywhere on the planet) and the reservoirs are slowly collapsing. The hum could be the rumble of shrinking aquifers. If you worry about this, drink beer instead. I'm having one as I write this just in case.

4. James Thurber highlighted the danger of electricity leaking from unused outlets in his story "The Car We Had To Push." With the advent of compact fluorescents and increased environmental awareness, more and more outlets and light sockets are going wanting, leading to a 60-cycle hum that is common around buildings. Wear rubber-soled shoes, is my suggestion.

5. It could also be a legacy of the ASARCO smelter pollution. Arsenic and other toxic elements might combine in audiotropic reactions with silica and other common rock-forming compounds. What you are hearing is the slow march of poison down towards our water supply.

6. Lastly, consider the aging demographics of our island. More people are suffering from buildups of ear wax, leading to low-frequency ringing in the ears. It's a form of tinnitus. Look it up.

None of these effects is very dangerous, except maybe the cosmic radiation that could destroy all life in the solar system, and the buildup of ear wax that has already taken the lives of two islanders (I've been told). One guy had his ear blown completely off. But I don't worry about that; instead, I worry about all the treasures that are hidden on Vashon and whether someone else will find them before I do.

The treasures I refer to are cataloged in a book I already mentioned, *Codex Benthos*, by Cecil Benthos, PhD. It's the first ever (and possibly last ever) catalog of lost mines, buried treasures, unsolved mysteries, and unexplained oddities on Vashon and Maury islands. Copies should be available at local bookstores. Make a fuss if they don't have one, or you can always order one online.

Looking for buried treasures, real and otherwise, is always great fun, and it's actually why I got into the field of geology. I first played around with the idea of being an archaeologist (no jobs and little pay), then a chemist (I'd have to study differential equations and I wasn't up for that), a lawyer (a brief prepubescent fling with the dark side that I outgrew in middle school), and finally an engineer (differential equations, ugh, they're everywhere). Geology kept me outside, made me look like Indiana Jones, and I was doing good for our great nation by finding precious metals that were needed for industry. I could save America by going hiking!!

The best part of it all is the search. We use all kinds of geophysical and geochemical tools, as well as drilling rigs and dynamite, to hunt for the treasures of the Earth. It's like being an archaeologist, only you get to blow up things and keep the treasure. And I was born with exceptional finding skills. You name it, I could find it, even if it didn't exist.

I attribute part of my skills to being educated with an exceptional group of geology students. The Class of 1974 at the University of Missouri-Rolla included, by all accounts, the most talented and creative geology students ever seen in the history of the school.

If you've never heard of this school, it's understandable because they keep changing their name. It was founded in 1870 as the Missouri School of Mines, or MSM. Shortly before I got there, they were absorbed by the University of Missouri system and became the University of Missouri-Rolla, or UMR. Recently, they've morphed again into the Missouri University of Science and Technology, or MUST. I don't know of another single school that has had such a hard time figuring out what to call itself.

On the other hand, my other alma mater, the Colorado School of Mines (or CSM), has been known by that name since 1874. They never once thought of changing their moniker, which suggests to me that either they are oblivious to the rape-and-pillage image of mining held by the general public, or they just don't care. It doesn't seem to matter; CSM is highly regarded worldwide as a leading school in all kinds of science and engineering, and they truly deserve that, but MSM/UMR/MUST is just as good a school. More people know about CSM, and I assume it's because they've never changed their name. It's just less confusing.

Being clever at finding things can also come in useful at times, particularly if you have "credentials." Sometimes, it doesn't take much to qualify as credentials. In 1973, for example, I accompanied a group of private detectives from Oklahoma City, headed by a man named Glenn Magill, on a search for the Lost Dutchman Mine. These people actually invited me because I was an "expert," which in this case meant a geology student still a year away from graduating and having no practical experience whatsoever. I guess that compared to the private detectives, I was an expert in geology and mining.

The Lost Dutchman is probably the most famous lost mine in the lower 48 states, partly because it's supposedly located in the scenic Superstition Mountains, a short drive from Phoenix. The Superstitions are readily accessible, a great place to go hiking, and just scary enough to interest lost mine hunters and other wackos. In true wild-west fashion, businesses all around the area cater to the treasure-hunting tourist trade. You can't imagine how many people buy into it.

In search of the Lost Dutchman.

If you want to read a historical account of my experience, by which I mean a largely fictional version that prompted me to consult an attorney, find a copy of the book *The Killer Mountains*, by Curt Gentry. Make sure you get the 1973 printing with the Epilogue, and you'll find me on page 237. On the book's cover, it says that *The Killer Mountains* is the "Great story of the last search for the Lost Dutchman Mine." Yeah, right.

But running around the Superstitions with a bunch of naïve security experts was a hoot, I have to say. They didn't know much about camping (we packed in steaks and beer on horseback), but they could party when they wanted. And my minimal "credentials" resulted in my very first citation in the literature. Thankfully, it was the last citation of that type.

There are supposed to be ghosts in the Superstition Mountains, which is how I am going to transition into this next topic: Ghosts. Now a lot of scientists will discount the idea that ghosts exist, mainly because there is no proof of them. Science does, after all, require all hypotheses to be validated through testing, by which I mean collecting data and observations that either prove the truth of the hypothesis or disprove all others. No one has ever shown, with data that can be reproduced, that ghosts exist.

The absence of any proof that ghosts exist doesn't stop well-meaning and otherwise sane individuals from both believing in them and looking for them just about anywhere you can imagine. Clearly, the best places to look for ghosts are where people used to live, and the more people the better. Other good places to look include where crimes have occurred (which theoretically should include many automobiles if you include passionate indiscretions and traffic violations), burial grounds (it takes dying to produce ghosts), and famous old buildings. Bridges also work, and basements, and dark creepy places in the woods. Ghosts can also possess certain people and animals. Cats are prone to possession, but dogs are generally safe because they are more "single-minded."

As you might guess, there are also ghosts on Vashon. I've already mentioned the ghost that used to haunt the space that was the Gusto Girls restaurant, and may still be there. In *Codex Benthos*, there are stories of other ghosts including one in the bathroom behind the Heron's Nest. I think all you'd have to do to find a ghost on Vashon is to hang out late at night at any of the numerous historic sites, including many of the older houses and sites of Indian encampments. Of course, the cemetery is always a good prospect, as is the Pt. Robinson lighthouse, the old coffee roastery, and maybe even the high school. Vashon has also been host to a few murders, but those crime scenes were in private dwellings, and most of the present residents do not offer after-hours tours. I don't know why, but people usually look for ghosts in the dark, possibly because ghosts, like vampires, sleep during the day.

UFO watching is also a nighttime activity, and Vashon is famous worldwide among UFO researchers. There have been three well-documented sightings on or near Vashon over the years, and *Codex Benthos* contains complete accounts of all three. The most famous is the Maury Island sighting of 1947. I refer you to *Codex Benthos* for the whole story; the following account comes from that source.

On June 21, 1947, Harold Dahl was piloting a boat and salvaging logs just south of Maury Island with his son, two crewmen, and his dog. It was there that Dahl and the others spotted six doughnut-shaped disks hovering overhead. Dahl later reported that the objects were about 100 feet in diameter and had a bright metallic appearance. One was wobbling and appeared to be trouble. It dropped to about 500 feet above the water and was accompanied by the other disks that appeared to be providing some kind of assistance. After some sort of explosion, the foundering disk ejected hot debris that resembled cooled lava and fell in large flakes. The falling debris injured Dahl's son and killed the dog. Afterward, the disks rose rapidly and flew off.

Dahl and his crew headed to the shore where he stopped to assess the damage and take photos. Gathering up some of the debris, he proceeded to Tacoma, where his son was taken to a hospital for first aid. The dog's body was buried at sea on the return trip.

Dahl reported the incident to Fred Crisman, who was the harbor patrol supervisor, but Crisman did not believe him. Nevertheless, Crisman went to the location that Dahl described and recovered more of the debris, which he described as being there in large quantities. While picking up some of the debris, Crisman spotted another disk that he said dropped more.

The next morning, a man arrived at the Dahl home and invited him to breakfast at a nearby diner. Dahl described the man as tall, imposing, and wearing a black suit. He drove a 1947 Buick, and Dahl assumed he was a military or government official. Over breakfast, the man in black revealed that he knew details about the sighting that had not been publicly available, and he also gave Dahl a warning. Dahl was told he was not supposed to see what he had seen and that he should not discuss it with anyone.

This poster says it all.

Three days later, a former military aviator and federal marshal named Kenneth Arnold saw nine similar disks flying across the face of Mt. Rainier. This sighting led to the coining of the term "flying saucer" and was widely reported in the press. Arnold was interviewed by local and national journalists, including Edward R. Murrow, and his account made headlines around the world. He was also interviewed by 1st Lt. Frank Brown and Capt. William Davidson, both from Hamilton Field in California. Oddly, 16 other sightings were reported of similar objects that same day at other sites in Washington, Oregon, and Idaho. Three of the sightings were in Seattle. Ten of them were in Washington State. The June 24th sighting by Arnold is commonly considered the "first" UFO sighting, but the Maury incident predates it by three days.

United Airlines Capt. E. J. Smith was a friend of Kenneth Arnold, but was skeptical of Arnold's story until July 4 of that year. On a flight from Boise to Tacoma, Smith noticed a formation of saucer-shaped objects near his aircraft. Capt. Smith, Co-Pilot Ralph Stevens and Stewardess Marty Morrow all reported they saw the objects.

Ray Palmer, the editor of *Amazing Stories*, contacted Arnold and asked him to investigate the Maury Island story. Arnold agreed, and contacted his friend Capt. Smith for help. Arnold, Smith, and the two military officers who had interviewed Arnold, Capt. Davidson and 1st Lt. Brown, met Harold Dahl at the Winthrop Hotel on July 31.

Arnold, in his book "The Coming of the Saucers," states that it was about midnight when the interview ended. Davidson and Brown called for a command car to pick them up, as they seemed to be in a hurry to return to Hamilton Field. It was Air Force Day, the inauguration day of the separation of the Air Force from the Army, and all planes were needed. Just as the command car pulled up in front of the hotel, Fred Crisman arrived and took a large cornflakes box out of his trunk, presenting it to the officers. Arnold states that the material inside the box looked a lot like the "slag" samples they had in their room, which had been collected from the beach.

The next morning, Arnold received a call from Crisman informing him that the radio was reporting news of a B-25 bomber that had exploded and crashed twenty minutes after takeoff from McChord Field. The bomber had crashed near Kelso, Washington, and was the same plane that was on its way to California with Davidson, Brown, and the box of extraterrestrial debris. There were survivors, but Davidson and Brown were not among them.

There were rumors at the time that the aircraft was under guard every minute it was at McChord Field, which was thought to be unusual, and there were also rumors the plane was sabotaged or shot down. The *Tacoma Times* printed a story about the crash, stating that sabotage was hinted and that the plane may have held secrets to the flying disk mystery. Written by Paul Lance, the article stated the plane had been sabotaged to prevent shipment of "flying disk fragments" to California for analysis. Oddly, Paul Lance died two weeks later of unknown causes. The cause of the plane crash was later determined to be a failure in the left engine.

An interesting coincidence in this case is that the Washington sightings occurred at almost the same time debris was first discovered in Roswell, New Mexico. The Roswell incident was first reported on July 8, but the crash site was discovered a few weeks before that.

That is the official history of the Maury UFO sighting. You can research this topic in any location and find the same account, which leaves you wondering what really happened. Was the whole thing a hoax? Even in those days, there were a few cameras around, so why did no one get a good picture? If such a thing were to happen today, the cell phone pictures would be on Facebook within minutes.

There are so many UFOs out here that we have to provide directions.

So, if you go ghost or UFO hunting, make sure and take your camera (or your cell phone), with and without flash, and some kind of recording device for sound. I tried once taking my cordless phone (I didn't go far), calling my own number (which was obviously busy), and using the answering machine to record ghostly sounds, but this didn't work so well. It also alarmed my wife and children. They began to wonder just what I learned when I was a geology student.

Which brings me back to the UMR class of 1974. My advisor and mentor from that time, Dr. S. Kerry Grant (we sometimes referred to him as Scary Grant), who unfortunately is now passed on, told me once that the 1974 graduates were the most creative and imaginative bunch he had ever seen. This was in about 1987, after he had ushered through 13 more classes. The newer kids were, according to Dr. Grant, a lot less creative, but also a lot quieter, respectful, and religious, and he didn't have to worry about them getting arrested or showing up in class with a hangover.

It's true that we were a rowdy bunch. I could write here about hopping trains and stealing Christmas trees (which we selflessly gave to deserving coeds), spelunking with beer, borrowing road signs, and assorted other forms of misconduct (none of which was a really serious crime), including raiding the girls' dorm and wearing stolen pantyhose over jeans on the main street after hours, but I don't want to embarrass my former classmates. Some of them currently have important high-level positions with large corporations and government agencies, and such revelations in print may not be welcome. So if you want a list, send your address and a hundred-dollar bill to me at the address in the front of this book.

Dr. Grant knew about these things, and he made a bet with me in my junior year. If I could graduate without ever getting arrested for public intoxication, indecent exposure, or resisting arrest, he'd give me an old wooden sign he had saved from the early days of the MSM Department of Geology and Geophysics that said (in hand-painted letters) "GEOLOGY DEPT."

I'm here to report that his sign is hanging in my office today. I know you miss the sign, Dr. Grant, but we miss you more.

Wrapping It Up: Things to Do with the Kids (besides yelling at them)

YOU MAY BE wondering why I saved this topic for last. It could be that I didn't think about the kids until after I had written everything else. Even if that were true, I'd never admit it here. Instead, I'd rather you believe (because it's true) that I saved it for last because it's my belief that everything in our lives, including reading this book, should be in preparation for helping the children.

Those of you who are already parents may have discovered that the most important role you will play in your life is simply being a good parent to your children. All other tasks pale in comparison, and everything you do should be done with that role in mind. If you don't have any kids, you're not off the hook because then you must be a good example for the children of others.

If you stand back for a moment and view the bigger picture of mankind and life on our planet, it's not always a pretty picture. Our kids will be inheriting an incredible mess, and so that's why I think it's important to do what we can to improve things now. One way to do that is to always look for problem solutions that maximize future benefits for the children rather than to benefit you or some other short-term goal. That way, you will *always* be making the right decision for mankind and the environment. You will choose conservation because it's good for future generations. You will choose clean air, clean water, good beer, economic justice, and saving endangered species because it's good for the planet, and what's good for the planet is good for our children.

It is when we don't consider the impacts of our actions, both short- and long-term, that we are counted as thoughtless and selfish. Humans can be just as greedy and ruthless as a school of piranhas. God knows I've tried. But the difference is that we have the ability (whether we use it or not) to predict the future based upon current trends and to understand our place in the universe. The piranhas don't know if another swimmer is going to take a dip, but we can see the bigger picture. If we don't use our gifts, then we might as well not have them.

What Vashon can offer the good parent is lots of opportunities to both teach and have fun with your kids, especially if they are younger and not yet embarrassed to be seen with you. For example, something as simple as a walk on the beach can be loads of fun for little ones as well as educational. I used to take my kiddos for walks and each time we'd make a point of bringing back some of the trash that was strewn in the woods. They learned about litter at the same time they were identifying trees and watching for fossils or butterflies.

Now that my own children are grown (and one is a parent herself), I have formulated five basic rules for being a good parent. I have never before stated these rules, much less offered them in print, so my own children may find them to be interesting reading. The rules are quite simple, but following them is not always simple and is never easy. If it were easy, we'd all be good parents.

Rule No. 1: Always love your child as much as you can. I know this can be a challenge, especially after they turn 13. Just grit your teeth and love your child. Nothing is more important.

Rule No. 2: Life is all about attitude. Be strong in the face of adversity, and work to solve problems rather than create them. Be slow to anger, quick to laugh, and always ready for adventure. Show your children how to do this by example.

Rule No. 3: As I said above, for all choices that you have to make, think about how your choice will affect the children of the world. If you always consider both short- and long-term impacts, then you'll be a good steward of the planet that your children will inherit.

Rule No. 4: Avoid pressures from society and from your child's peers. For example, only allow one television and one computer in the house, locate them someplace central (such as in the family room), and limit their use. Never allow a TV in a bedroom (especially your own unless you are no longer interested in romance). And you don't need all of those other technological devices, including the ones with the little screens that people keep poking. There are a lot more things to worry about that stem partly from societal pressures and the media, including alcohol and drug use, inappropriate sexual activity, disrespectful behavior, voting Republican, and so on. It's important to remember that **you** are responsible for teaching your children, not NBC, Microsoft, or World of Warcraft.

Rule No. 5: Spend as much time with your kids as you can. This advice also works for dogs, and sometimes the similarity is frightening, but I can assure you that it will pay off in the long run. For example, when the kids are little, let them help you with chores. Let them help you with yard work and the laundry and afterwards take them for a hike or to a playground. Take them to museums and movies and historic sites and zoos. Education is important, but so is socialization and learning to take care of themselves and be a functioning part of the family.

Rule No. 6: Be prepared to add more rules. Kids don't come with owners manuals. Dads wouldn't read them anyway.

As the kids get older, you can also help them with school projects and scout projects and maybe even coach their sports team. Both of my kids excelled at sports. My daughter Katy became a synchronized swimmer and today coaches a team of award-winning swimmers. Her mother helped with that because it was their mother/daughter thing. I did the father/son thing with my son Nathaniel, who we signed up for several sports (of his choosing) including softball, soccer, and later lacrosse. He liked lacrosse because you could hit people with sticks and get away with it.

I went to a lot of games, but only once did I get more intimately involved, and that was when Nathaniel was about ten years old and we signed him up for softball at the YMCA. I took him to the first practice and the coach, a large strapping man who knew everything there was to know about all sports, asked for volunteers to be "assistant coaches." I was the lone dad standing there with three mothers, and so I had no choice but to volunteer. My son was proud of me, but I was terrified, because as a child I was always small for my grade (mainly because I just barely made the cutoff for kindergarten) and my family was not into sports. I played every game poorly and didn't know the rules for most. The other kids usually made fun of me and didn't want me on their team. To meet this coaching challenge, I first went to the library to find a book on the rules of baseball.

When the time came for Nate's first game, I was tapped to be the third-base coach. My aunt and uncle from San Diego were in the audience, and they were huge fans of the Padres and quite knowledgeable about the game. From my outpost at third base, I think I actually heard Uncle Carl yelling something about the infield fly rule, whatever that is, but I was out there without a clue of what to do. The real coach sensed this and tried to feed me a few tips from the dugout as the kids were running the bases. This worked for the first two kids who made it to third base, but the third one was tagged out after I sent him to home plate. It was clearly my fault, and I felt like I was in 7th grade again. In retrospect, it was a ghost I had to exorcise, and it showed my son that I am not perfect. Not that he didn't already know that.

Science fairs were a lot easier for me. I helped both of my children with science fair projects beginning as early as first grade, when Katy did a project comparing the sizes of popped kernels of different brands of popcorn. Orville Reddenbacher's was the best, but we got to eat them all. I can truly say that the entire family enjoyed her project.

Even though I was a science nerd and rock collector from as early as first grade, my parents helped me with my projects, too. I did projects on Indian mounds, photography through the microscope, and making kites. But my best science fair project was in 8th grade when my dad helped me build a Van de Graaff Generator.

I know it looks like there are too many letter A's in Graaff, but that is not so, nor is it a significant error to add an apostrophe to the letter A even when it is not intended to be indicative of the possessive tense. I've wanted to write a sentence like that for years.

You've probably seen one of these generators in an old Frankenstein movie. The Van de Graaff generator is an electrostatic generator that uses a moving belt to accumulate very high electrostatically stable voltages on a hollow metal globe on the top of a stand. Basically, it's a big metal ball from which large sparks emit, usually when you least expect them. It was invented in 1929 by American physicist Robert J. Van de Graaff, hence the name. My encyclopedia says that the potential differences achieved in modern Van de Graaff generators can reach five megavolts. I don't know what this means, but I do know that the sparks can be really long (six inches to a foot) but that they are static electricity, and so they don't pack much punch. If I was an electrical engineer, I'd say that they have a very high voltage, but a very low amperage, sort of like being sprayed with a squirt gun instead of a fire hose.

Talk about fun! A small electric motor (that you plugged into the wall socket) ran a rubber belt up and down a Lucite tube, on top of which was an aluminum sphere about 14 inches in diameter. And every so often...POW! A spark jumped from the sphere to whatever was closest. Usually, that was a ladle I had grounded to the base of the generator. But once during a demonstration in my 8th grade science class, it was a very fuzzy sweater being worn by a friend of mine whose name I think was Mark. Upon receiving the jolt, Mark jumped back and nearly landed on a cute girl (Stephanie) who was sitting behind him, leading to speculation among the other students (for days) as to Mark's actual intentions. The teacher, who did not have a science background and so was bereft of any passion for discovery, banned my generator from class. I nevertheless took a medal (second place) at the White Oak Junior High Science Fair.

As my senior year was winding down at Colerain High School in 1970, I donated the treasured generator to the science department of the high school. By then, the rubber belt was cracked and needed to be replaced, and there was a small dent in the sphere where another sparking episode resulted in a minor disturbance.

I gave it up reluctantly. I wish I had it now.

CPSIA information can be obtained at www.ICGtesting.com
Printed in the USA
BVOW071748180312

285445BV00001B/48/P